D0150377

Praying Beyond God's Ability

by
Roy H. Hicks, D.D.

HARRISON HOUSE
Tulsa, Oklahoma

Unless otherwise indicated,
all Scripture quotations are taken from
the King James Version of the Bible.

16th Printing
Over 72,000 in Print

Praying Beyond God's Ability
ISBN 0-89274-052-3
Copyright © 1977 by Roy H. Hicks, D.D.

P. O. Box 4113
San Marcos, California 92069

Published by Harrison House, Inc.
P. O. Box 35035
Tulsa, Oklahoma 74153

Contents

About The Book

If you're praying more and enjoying it less — largely because so many petitions seem to command no direct answer — this book by Roy Hicks, Sr. may be "just what the doctor orders." It will help you sharpen your intercession by correcting sloppy attitudes and actions relative to prayer.

Dr. Hicks emphasizes that prayer need not be a matter of hit or miss — with the petitioner missing more than he hits. The author points out as improper the circumstance that many Christians remain lazily content with a small percentage of answers to a large volume of prayers.

Every chapter of this book is freighted with significant teaching, truths which can dramatically turn around an ineffective prayer life. However, the chapters which minister most to me — and that deal with basics which we dare not minimize or ignore — are "Praying Beyond God's Ability" and "Principle not Formula." Here we find fresh illumination of timeless Biblical truths. Author Hicks' instructions, if followed, may result in less shot-gun petitioning on believers' parts but virtually guarantee more prayers on target, and accordingly more recognizable answers.

Unless you're praying simply for the sake of praying — an unbiblical motive if there ever was one — you want answers to the requests you make known to God. A study of and practice of the principles here expressed shouldn't make you pray less and enjoy it more but will embolden you to pray more in quality as well as in quantity with the consequences that "the effectual fervent prayer of a righteous man availeth much" (James 5:16).

—Dr. Raymond L. Cox

Introduction

This is not a book on prayer, how to pray, the need to pray . . . or even on great answers to prayer. Library shelves are full of good books on these subjects. This is a book which I trust will force us to face the reality of unanswered prayers and endeavor to do something about it.

Praying Beyond God's Ability, The Enigma of Unanswered Prayer, will discuss a multitude of errors on prayer and faith. We are so quick to relate the answers to prayer, but so reluctant to face the failures.

Never in the history of the church has there been a time when the body of Christ has been more exposed to the faith message than it is today. It has had constant exposure through radio, television, books and periodicals . . . in addition to churches and city wide meetings. Coinciding with this are the many frustrated and baffled Christians who are attempting to practice all they have heard . . . but with little success.

While God is faithful to honor His Word, His honor will not allow Him to break the higher laws of man's will and choice. God will not save, heal, or deliver a man against his will regardless of how hard and fervently we pray.

We, as Christians, seem to be more interested in getting our hands into His honey-jar, than we are to have His hand on our lives. While we delight in having God doing our bidding . . . we cringe at doing His bidding. We expect His ear to be open to our cry . . . but close ours to His will for our lives.

God loves us, cares for us, and wants us to have the desires of our hearts. Prayer and faith principles will work, attested to by millions. I pray the reading and practicing of what is contained herein will produce an even greater relationship to our Father, through Jesus Christ His Son, by the person of the Holy Spirit.

— Dr. Roy H. Hicks

1

Praying Beyond God's Ability

Praying beyond God's ability is praying a prayer that elicits from God the answer, "I am sorry I can't do that for you, even if I wanted to." The immediate reaction of many people could almost be one of resentment that the author would suggest such an absurdity as the title of this book. Haven't we heard all of our lives that there is nothing, absolutely nothing, that God cannot do? Do not the Scriptures teach that with God all things are possible? (Mark 9:23). About the time we get comfortable in our cliches someone will say something like, "Could God make a rock so big He couldn't lift it?" Then we quickly turn away, change the subject, or busy ourselves otherwise.

It is very easy for Bible lovers to quote lengthy passages concerning God's great ability . . . and to believe it with all of their hearts, then go on through life comparatively undisturbed by unanswered prayers and unmoved mountains, desiring not to question and seek answers as to why their prayers went unanswered and the mountains remained. Should we hesitate to question the statement, "All things are possible," for fear we will tread where angels fear to tread? Or do we need to thoroughly understand what is the scriptural meaning of that statement? Is it possible for God to answer if someone were to pray, "God make the devil bigger and more powerful than you are"? I get cold chills just thinking what might happen if God would answer that prayer. You would quickly reply, "That is impossible." God always was, and is. Past, present and future . . . unchangeable in his omnipotent power. So such a prayer would be impossible in the light of God's omnipotence.

Keep in mind, in thinking about affairs that relate to this life, that when Jesus said, "all things are possible," He meant that within certain limitations and boundaries. What are those limitations and boundaries? Inasmuch as the Bible uses the relationship of Father and Son or the Father and His family, let us receive some light and understanding from this similitude that will guide us to a better comprehension about the subject of unanswered prayer.

Is it possible for an earthly father to teach his one-year old son to guide a great complex corporation? No. Simply because the child is only an infant . . . still learning the primary functions of life. The age of the child, and his capacity, will dictate the father's ability to communicate to, and do things for, his son. Will not also common sense exercise control over the father's desires to do for his son? Would he give his young son a poisonous snake or any other dangerous, harmful object in answer to his request? Someone might remark that we know all about what an earthly father can or cannot do . . . but we are talking about a supreme God who can do anything! So get on with it! But we can't move on to the understanding of great and mighty things without understanding the foundation on which they rest. God is our Father and we are His children, and that is an unchangeable fact. Praying beyond God's ability is not just based on who He is, but also on who we are, our relationship to Him and the degree of our maturity.

One of the greatest mistakes we make is in trying to get God to answer prayer that is not in the best interest of *everyone* concerned. For God to completely and continually answer one person's selfish prayers would set him up higher than God. It would put God in the awkward position of eventually, in order to answer that person's prayer, perhaps making a rock too big for Him to lift! If God could allow a wife to completely carry her husband spiritually, by her prayer life and faith's confession, would that man become a great leader with powerful influence? No, because his life style, and his will, not being submitted under control of the Spirit in a personal relationship, would not bring glory to God, nor develop and mature that person. Rather, the wife would become as God to him.

Praying beyond God's ability, or praying beyond the limitations that exist, because we are his children, is a great principle that should *bless us* rather than l*imit us*. God always wants to do what is best for us. He looks ahead to see how that answered prayer will not only abound to our good, but also to the welfare of His overall kingdom. Not all prayers keep God's good uppermost, nor do they seek to bless His kingdom.

Somehow, the shameful fact of man's pride must fit into the limitations of prayer. This word, pride, probably more than any other word, prevents God from being good to us and hinders many answers to our prayers. Even before He would greatly desire to give us what we are presently asking for, He is concerned about the pride that is already present. That pride may be a result of the last prayer He answered for us. If He answers another one, He will do irreparable damage to our spiritual relationship with Him, and to His overall Kingdom.

Our ability to receive from God has a great bearing on His desire and ability to answer our prayers. God can only trust us with a very small portion of His power and ability to work miracles because of the human pride factor. God has difficulty in finding people He can trust. Remember, it was pride that caused rebellion in heaven originally. God doesn't want you to be in danger of falling because of the same reason that Lucifer fell (Ezekiel 28:17).

In the history of the church, some persons have received great power to work miracles. When this occurs, many times the people who see these miracles will elevate the person being used by the Lord to a higher plane than God Himself . . . and hold them in reverence and wonder, thereby causing that person who was put on a pedestal to be in danger of falling.

The boundaries that determine God's ability to do, or not do, for His children, have already been established by His first gift to us. This is higher in priority than the answer to your prayers. God's greatest gift to man, as a human being, is man's will. His ability to choose to serve God . . . or choose to serve God's enemy — what a significant gift. Man took the greatest gift God ever bestowed and turned and used it against Him. By allowing man to choose, God limits Himself in what He can now do for man, by that gift of choice. Even though man can choose wrongly, it is still God's most significant gift to him. God would receive no pleasure from a person who was forced to stand before him as a robot, who had no alternative or choice and mechanically intone, "Hallelujah, hallelujah, praise God." We worship because we choose to worship, because it wells up from within our being and must be given expression. This gift of God in allowing us the ability to choose, a gift intended to bless us, now can become an instrument in our hands that will work against us. Because we are now free to choose, we can do so selfishly. The moment God hears a prayer that is prayed in this manner, He is reluctant to answer it. The reason for this? Because the pray-er has already abused the original gift, that of choice. Any prayer prayed stemming from the wrong motive cannot be answered in our best interest, because it promotes the wrong use of the will.

God intended our will to be a blessing, not a detriment. Doubtless, as you have been reading, you have questioned in your heart, "What about Israel's requesting

Samuel to give them a king as the other nations had —
this was not God's perfect will." In allowing them a king,
He was allowing their choice of rejecting Him. In so doing,
it cost them great heartache. In the future it would be
useless for them to cry out for help and mercy. God had
told Samuel to inform them about the troubles they would
have because of the subsequent rule of many evil kings.
Their prayers cannot be answered because they are *praying beyond God's ability*. They used His great gift, that of
their free will, wrongly, by choosing to ask selfishly. They
wanted to be as other heathen nations, instead of letting
God be their king.

Many people have wilfully chosen a marriage partner
against God's will, and thus have ended up in the misery
of being unequally yoked together. They knew it was
wrong to marry an unbeliever. God allowed it, because
they were given a choice, their free will was allowed.
Then when troubles came, as God said they would, their
prayers were beyond God's ability to answer, because
they violated His original gift of will wrongly, by going
against His Word. There is no easy way out (II Corinthians 6:14), except they can now repent and seek forgiveness for their gross error and be reinstated in God's mercy
and forgiveness. By now children may have been born
to that marriage, which complicates it even more, and
Solomon himself could not sort out the confused lines
resulting from this wrong use of their will.

God has a perfect will for our lives. We must seek
that will and plan and it must have priority in our lives.
He cannot do for us *rightly* if we choose *wrongly*. His
highest will is for our eternal good. One would be as a fool
not to seek it. Matthew 6:33 says, "But seek ye first the
kingdom of God, and his righteousness; and all these
things shall be added unto you." Yet thousands of prayers
are prayed selfishly; thus it is beyond God's ability to

answer them for everybody's welfare and the best interest of God's kingdom.

Let me illustrate the confusion that comes from abusing the gift of choice. A man could see his neighbor living in a costly mansion, driving expensive limousines, eating gourmet food, and he would jealously, enviously desire the same things. Actually, he could be coveting. While it is not wrong to want to prosper, the wrong motive for prospering could easily be an abuse of God's gift to him, that of his free will. This envious man could sell all he had, borrow all he could, and invest everything he had to go into business to make money for himself. He is doing this because others have gained great wealth and prospered. He is not seeking God's perfect plan for his life. He is not seeking relationship. He is seeking wealth at any cost. God granted him the free will of choice. Because his motives are wrong, he becomes greatly discouraged because his prayers are not being answered and he is about to lose all his investment.

One such man heard a faith teacher preach a great sermon on prosperity. He promptly sold all that he had and invested his money very unwisely and ended up losing everything. He was only a baby Christian, a novice. He went beyond his relationship and faith — thus he failed. All faith teachers and ministers would do well to present all of the truth and not just a portion. Not all of the body of Christ has the same function or same purposes. We are not all meant to be wealthy businessmen. Some are destined to be missionaries, some teachers who will teach in poor areas at great sacrifice, yet be happy. Some are meant to be lawyers, doctors, laborers, etc. We should allow for each man to find his proper gift (Romans 12), and so operate without condemnation being heaped upon him by hearing a prosperity message that caused him to take a step beyond his gifts.

A common occurrence will illustrate the point of praying beyond God's ability. Two teams are coming together to meet in competition. There are Christians on both sides. You will have to appreciate the deep emotions some people have in the sports contest to understand the fervency with which the prayers ascend to the throne of God from combatants on both sides. "Lord, help us to win this game!" Perhaps as these prayers ascend to God's throne, He just chuckles and says, "May the best team win."

Praying beyond God's ability can be illustrated by talking about the time factor. In one chapter I have written about the need for time to mature, time to heal, etc. Here we contrast time in relationship to all that God can, someday, do for us that He cannot do now. God's gift of time is placed alongside His gift of choice. We have twenty-four hours a day, not 25. We have seventy or eighty years, not one hundred and seventy. There is a time for a man to be born . . . and a time to die. He does all of these things within that time slot allotted for existence on earth. If he is born in the 20th century, God does not judge Him for the first century. If he is one year old, God does not judge him as He would one who had lived for fifty years. Therefore God's ability to answer some prayers is closely related to our age and the day in which we are living.

A good example of this is when people are seeking God's will for their lives. They are greatly burdened about the future. They are now in training, for example, for the ministry. They have three more years before they are prepared to make a major change. They are greatly exercised as to where they will go and what they will be doing. They are, at the present time, doing God's will in studying His word and preparing themselves. They are frustrating themselves by praying over something in the future that God doesn't intend to show them. The answer could greatly hinder what they are presently doing. There-fore, to pray about a time related factor that has no bear-ing on the present would put them in the category of praying beyond God's ability to help. Good advice to all is this: When you are doing God's will, do not seek His will . . . you are already doing it. Just *trust* Him, and when the time comes, He will show you what you need to know.

A frail, elderly man can be possessed with a burning desire to train and go to the mission field, or pastor a large church. God cannot answer such a prayer because of his advanced age. He should have prepared and prayed that prayer in his youth. There is a time for everything. Do not pray beyond God's ability to do either that which is behind you, or too far ahead of you.

The Word teaches that God is no respector of per-sons. History has witnessed much heartache because of partiality among men. This is especially true in a home where the parents have singled out just one of the chil-ren on whom they have showered all of their affection. Not only did it cause deep-seated resentment and heart-ache in the neglected child, but the partiality spoiled the one who received all of the attention. Thus, it is beyond God's ability to answer some prayers because in answer-ing them it would make him a respecter of persons.

God's ability to answer our prayers is clearly taught in the Word. Let us keep our prayers within that boun-dary. God is not in the business of making rocks so big that He cannot lift them!

2

Principles of Prayer

*If you hem your morning with prayer you are not
so likely to come unraveled as the day wears on.*

M. Johnson

In Luke 11:1 the disciples asked the Lord Jesus to
teach them how to pray as John also taught his disciples.
It was at this time that Jesus taught what is commonly
known as the "Lord's Prayer" . . . or what we will now
call the "Prayer Principle." We will talk about that principle first.

Webster has defined the word "principle" as the ultimate source, origin, or cause of something, fundamental
truth, law, doctrine as its first definition. Volumes have
been written concerning the subject of "how" to pray,
the "power" of prayer, praying "effectively," and so on,
and on. Prayer and its results cannot be over-emphasized.
Great men prayed and their prayers were answered. *I am
not so concerned about God's people misunderstanding
the power of prayer, as I am about their frustrations over
unanswered prayers!*

Let us begin by addressing ourselves to the initial,
basic subject — the misconception or misunderstanding
that many people have of what God is saying about the
Principle of Prayer, and what we interpret to be the
Methodology of Prayer . . . which, eventually, could be in

danger of deteriorating into mere formula. (See chapter on Formula.)

If Jesus is teaching formula and phraseology in the Lord's Prayer, then He didn't practice what He taught! We have no record that He ever used the "Our Father which art in Heaven" wording again. (Luke and Matthew record the same incident.) Nor did he always pray in secret, shutting the door behind Him. What He did teach us was that prayer is addressed to the Father; with worship first; submission to God's will second; necessities of life taken care of third; forgiveness fourth; and complete deliverance from evil fifth.

As we deal with these principles, try to recall some of your prayers that went unanswered and see if you "touched all the bases" or if you were "tagged out" because you didn't obey all the rules.

The first principle of prayer is worship. Many people miss touching this base. John 9:31 says, "Now we know that God heareth not sinners; but if any man be a worshipper of God, and doeth his will, him he heareth." Jesus so beautifully illustrated this in His public prayers. Matthew 11:25, "Oh, Father, Lord of heaven . . ." John 11:41, "Father, I thank thee . . ." John 17:1, "Father, the hour is come; glorify thy Son, that thy Son also may glorify thee." Father is used, not so much to indicate child to father, but to establish a relationship.

True worship of God is contingent on our relationship with God. If the significance of true worship could be condensed into two words, they would be "Abba, Father." Abba is a term that denotes great affection. Some of the last words uttered by John Wesley were, "I'll praise Him, I'll praise Him."

Millions of people pray every day. Millions of prayers go unanswered daily because the relationship is not there . . . even if the word "Father" is repeated. Relationship with the Father is based on the love we have for Jesus. John 8:42, "Jesus said unto them, If God were your Father, ye would love me . . ." Really loving Jesus will take us out of the superficial, shallow realm of mere religion, into the deep, full flow of a relationship with the Father.

So often we are too long on prayers, and too short on worship. Worship of the Father, based on relationship, clearly defines the difference between praise and worship. There are many people who vocalize praise, and this is comely (beautiful). But true worship involves the total man — spirit, soul, and body. Merrill Johnson said, "God hears the heart without words, but never words without heart."

When Jesus acknowledged God as His father, He was wholly conscious of the Father. I suspect that many times, especially in a church service, when the leader calls upon us to praise the Lord together, that we enter into praise vocally, but our minds are flitting about, thinking about a great variety of subjects, (not the least of which is our stomachs, especially if it is getting close to the noon hour).

Complete, true worship only ascends to the Father as you have ability to keep your mind (imaginations) on Him. John 4:23, 24 describes spiritual, truthful worshippers as those who worship God in spirit and in truth. The Father said He would seek those who worship Him in spirit and in truth. It is far better to have *Him seeking you* — than to have *you seeking Him!* He always knows where you are! The sad *truth* of the matter is that so many are guilty of being neither in spirit nor in truth! The truth is that, while we were in a stance of worship, we were guilty of thinking of a host of other things. Perhaps we even focused on our problems rather than on God, our Father. Prayer is more than "needs" relying on "omnipotence," it is worship.

It has been the author's privilege to act on something God said to him. This was, "Teach my people that when they come to worship me, to bring their imaginations (minds) with them. It gives me no pleasure when my people come before me, but their minds are somewhere else." Many times people have come to me after a service when we have led a congregation in a spiritual journey to the throne of God to worship Him, and have said, "I tried to do as you said and I couldn't." Others have said, "I was afraid to go." While some have had to continue to strive with their minds in the imagination realm for weeks before they could successfully go before the throne and worship Him totally as their Father, others have had no difficulty and immediately receive great blessings.*

If your angel could appear unto you and give you significant advice, he would probably repeat the same thing which was one of the last recorded words of an angel, "Worship God" (Revelations 22:9). This revival has ushered in a new era of spiritual worship. People, in their prayers, usually want *"things."* God wants *us.* A home run is wasted if you miss the first base.

The second principle, established in the Lord's prayer, is complete submission to God. "Thy Kingdom come, thy will be done." Millions of prayers go unanswered because we do not touch this base. Many people think that Jesus almost missed this one when He prayed, "If it be possible let this cup pass from me." But he went on to touch this base when He declared, "Not my will, but thine be done." True, whole-hearted submission to God is a sincere desire for God's overall benefit and glory rather than our own.

*See chapter on imaginations.

We are all prone to be very selfish. Recently someone came to me very upset about an unanswered prayer. After delving into the matter, I discovered the motive they had in wanting the answer to their prayer was that they might prove their spirituality before someone else! Many pastors do not have success because of wrong motives. A larger church, in their opinion, would prove to all that they really are good preachers . . . the public just doesn't know it yet.

True submission to God can usually be measured by one's submission to earthly authority. True humility is found in submission (I Peter 5:5, 6). The so-called independent spirit is always recognizable by its lack of submission to authority. Such a spirit only wants to be surrounded by people it can control, people who will do its every bidding. Be sure you are touching this often-missed base of complete submission to God and to His will for your life.

The third principle established in the Lord's prayer is one for daily provision, asking for your *daily* need — bread. What am I asking for as I pray for this necessity? Is it earthly bread? If it is, then we must ignore Matthew 6:33, "Seek ye first . . .". In Matthew 6:31 we are to take no thought of what we shall eat or drink, or with what we shall be clothed!

Satan tried to get Jesus to sin by taking thought of the bread one eats when his physical body is hungering (Matthew 4:1-4). Our *daily bread* is clearly defined in John 6:35-58. Our daily bread is Jesus, the Son of God, who is to be the true worshipper's *daily diet*. Sunday partaking is not enough. Every other day is not enough. Only that which we partake of daily is enough to get us through that day.

Millions of prayers go unanswered because the prayers are so emaciated and weak from lack of food that their prayers are too feeble to be heard. "For the children are come to the birth and there is not strength to bring forth" (II Kings 19:3b). Vigorous, forceful prayers are prayed by vigorous, healthy people who feed themselves with that Bread that came down from heaven. How do I feast on Jesus? The analogy of bread is used here because it is a physical act. I always prepare to eat bread. I also prepare to feed my spirit by partaking of the things of God, by reading the Word, by praying, and in worship I partake of the bread of God.

Jesus said in Matthew 4:4, "Man shall not live by bread (earthly) alone, but by every word (rhema) that proceedeth out of the mouth of God." Rhema is a Greek word that conveys the picture of one quoting the Word, speaking or singing the Word. If you haven't been touching this base, stop, partake of the living Bread . . . and then continue on.

The next principle to consider in the Lord's prayer is the principle of forgiveness. In every great prayer context forgiveness is mentioned. In the principle of prayer (Matthew 6:15), "But if ye forgive not men their trespasses neither will your Father forgive your trespasses." In the principle of faith, Mark 11:25a, "When ye stand praying, forgive." In faith increase, Luke 17:4, "And if he trespass against thee seven times in a day, and seven times in a day turn again to thee saying, I repent; thou shalt forgive him." And in binding and loosing, Matthew 18:35, "So likewise shall my heavenly Father do also unto you, if ye from your hearts forgive not every one his brother their trespasses."

We certainly want our prayers answered, our faith increased, and to have the power to bind and to loose . . . but do we want to have a forgiving spirit? The best illustration I have heard of this is in a story related to me by a pastor. There was a lady who came to him for counsel. She was greatly agitated. The reason for her agitation was that she had been praying for her husband to get saved. She had truly and sincerely done everything she knew to do in having faith and believing, and had searched her heart to be sure there was nothing standing in the way. There was a note of desperation in her voice when she said to her pastor, "I have done all I know to do. Now you tell me why he isn't saved!" The pastor knew the lady — knew her life and that she was a good woman. For a moment he did not have the answer. Then they bowed their heads to pray and seek the Father; and when they finished, the pastor said, "Sister, I only get one word — the word forgiveness. Will you go home and pray and seek the Lord for something, even delving back in the past, that you have not forgiven?"

The following day she called the pastor, and he recognized the note of joy and relief in her voice immediately. She told him that, as she followed his counsel and asked the Lord to reveal even things she might have forgotten, He did just as she asked. He showed her a spirit of unforgiveness that she had carried in her heart since childhood when she had suffered affliction and illness. She said, "I have been having a wonderful time with the Lord, forgiving all those people I had held things against all of these years." It is not coincidence that her husband gave his heart to the Lord the following Sunday!

It is so simple. Forgive and you will be forgiven. Forgiveness is a good spirit . . . Unforgiveness is a bad spirit. Forgiveness is not something to be earned. If someone trespasses against you, and you take out your displeasure on him for months — don't think you are giving him anything when you forgive him . . he earned it!! Jesus forgave you without your earning it. Be quick to forgive on that same basis!

Touching the base of forgiveness is so powerfully emphasized in the scripture and yet so simple. Many have been confused by hearing a speaker say that they need to go to everyone they need to forgive. This is only true if that person has aught against you (Matthew 5:23, 24). King David had sinned against God, Israel, Uriah and his relatives. Yet in Psalms 51:4 David declared that his need of forgiveness was from God. While one must be willing to go to another, there are times when great damage will be done by bringing something out in the open that will cause lasting trouble. It would have been more scriptural to just go to the Father and touch this vital base.

Some young tennis players were discovered by a deacon to be searching for lost balls in the carefully kept church grounds. In his concern for the church yard, he erected a sign which said, "Please Do Not Trespass." The next day he found another sign erected which said, "Forgive us our trespasses." The deacon removed his sign.

The Lord's prayer in Matthew 6:9-13 adds to the final principle of prayer, "deliver us from evil: For thine is the kingdom, and the power, and the glory, forever, Amen." This last base to be touched in our praying is the deliverance from evil . . . being free from evil influence . . . being servants to good and not to evil. This is accomplished by the acknowledgement of the power we have received by being in the Kingdom of God.

There are some people who seem to be frightened by the message of the kingdom of God. It is very simple. You are already in a kingdom — it is just a question of which one! Many churches do not have enough good, positive preaching and teaching on this vital subject. Many of God's people don't really know which kingdom they are in. One day they feel like they are in God's kingdom, and the next day the devil's.

Then there is always the potential danger of being bound in a kingdom of your own making, with all its limitations. Satan has only the power and influence you permit him to have. Rebuking, resisting him, and confession of your authority over him in Jesus' name is your right, privilege and power. To fail to do this will hinder your progress in God's kingdom. I am not what I feel, see, or sense. I am who God says I am! I must say this to the enemy. Also I must hear myself declare who I am and whom I serve.

Jesus built His church on the confession that He is the Christ, the Son of the Living God (Matthew 16:15-19). I entered the Kingdom of God by the great confession that Jesus is Lord (Romans 10:9, 10). I remain in and retain its kingdom power by this same confession.

The word declares, "Resist the devil and he will flee from you." This also means all the evil that assails me and tries to conquer me. The prayer to deliver us from evil is possible because "thine is the Kingdom, Oh Lord God of heaven and earth." The failure to live and walk in the kingdom is the reason for many of our unanswered prayers and for the frustrations we suffer. The words to this hymn summarize this truth very well:

> I walk with the King, hallelujah,
> I walk with the King, praise His name.
> No longer I roam; my soul faces home.
> I walk and I talk with the King.

God wants to answer our prayers. He cannot, because we do not walk with Him. He will not violate His laws and His principles. We have heard people talk about how many answers to prayer they had when they were first saved — but later on they failed to get answers. Why is this? It is very simple to understand. As a newborn babe in Christ, God didn't expect you to touch all of the bases of the prayer principle because you were not old enough in Him and had no time to learn. Now that you are of an age of spiritual maturity, God expects you to know the principles of prayer.

If you have had a prayer failure, stop right now and determine where you missed it. Ask God . . . He will talk to you. He will help you to learn from your experience of failure so you won't commit the same error again.

A producer offered an actor a hundred dollars if he could recite the Lord's prayer. He began, "Now I lay me down to sleep . . ." As he finished speaking the producer gave him the hundred dollars and said, "I am surprised you knew it so well!"

Our mistakes may not be that gross, but we all need to know more about that prayer than just the recital of it. Let us learn its principles and practice them in our own prayer life.

There are many man-made helps and devices to assist us in praying. There are prayer walls, prayer wheels, prayer rugs, prayer cloths, prayer beads, prayer chains, and you can even dial a prayer. But in all of this, keep uppermost the Lord's principles. Follow them closely, do them until they are formed into regular habits of prayer.

3

Faith Principles

Principle, defined by Webster is, "The ultimate source, origin or cause of something." Faith principles are spread throughout the Word in illustration and examples. Mark 11:22-24 seems to have condensed them for our better understanding. "And Jesus answering saith unto them, Have faith in God. (Have the God kind of faith.) For verily I say unto you, That whosoever shall say unto this mountain, Be thou removed, and be thou cast into the sea; and shall not doubt in his heart, but shall believe that those things which he saith shall come to pass; he shall have whatsoever he saith. Therefore I say unto you, What things soever ye desire, when ye pray, believe that ye receive them, and ye shall have them."

The context of this faith teaching takes place at the time Jesus cursed the fig tree and it withered away. The miracle produced great astonishment among the disciples — more than any other miracle that Jesus performed. I suppose the reason for their amazement could be that many miracles could be explained away by natural means, or duplicated, as in the case of Moses' rod when the Egyptian magicians were able to imitate his act of turning the rod into a serpent. But this miracle of the withered fig tree was, without a doubt in their mind, a direct result of the power of Jesus. The power of faith was operating so strongly in our Lord that just a word from him and an inanimate object responded by dying. In answer to Peter's reaction, the Lord explained to them this God-kind of faith and how it operates.

The principle of that God-kind of faith is just simply in saying a thing with your mouth, and believing it in your heart. Faith in the mouth and faith in the heart must come together . . . or it will not be the God-kind of faith. This subject is dealt with at length in my book on faith, Use It or Lose It. (May be secured from same publisher.)

Man kind of faith is usually only one half of the God kind of faith principle . . . The "saying" half. "I believe that God can do anything, but I don't know why this mountain hasn't moved!"; "I don't understand why I didn't get that promotion. I thought I did, but guess I didn't get it."; "I don't understand why I am not healed." Mountain moving faith (Mark 11.22-24) is what everyone wants, and everyone needs, but there are few who possess it. Most frustrations result as people try to move mountains too big for them. They fail and become discouraged and hesitate to try again. Some faith teachers fail to alert Christians to the fact that moving mountains requires such a God kind of faith that most people are not quite ready to attempt to move a mountain. The reason for this is that their relationship with God is so weak that, if they could move the mountain at all, instead of casting it into the sea, they would only budge it far enough to get it into someone else's back yard! That is not the God kind of faith.

Some, if they were able to move a mountain, would call out the news media to prove to the world their great ability to move a mountain, while others, if they could move a mountain, would buy one cheaply and move it somewhere else and build a house on it for profit! Then there are some of God's people who are not ready to move mountains. They are still building mountains. If they could move the one they have now, there would be two in its place tomorrow!

Does God want His children to be mountain movers? Yes! But he would far rather have them cease building them first. Fear is a mountain builder. So is doubt and worry. Jesus had a lot to say about it. In Matthew 8:26 He said, "Why are ye fearful, O ye of little faith?" The fear has to go before the faith will operate. We would rather have the faith operate first . . . and then we would deal with the fear later. The truth of the matter is that if we had the mountain moving faith first, we probably would enjoy it so much that we never would get around to dealing with fear. The same would be true with worry, doubt, etc.

We, as faith teachers, need to put the horse before the cart by being candidly honest. God wants us to be whole, healthy people in beautiful relationship with Him . . . far more than He wants us to be moving mountains at random.

The countless times of frustrations and feelings of deep condemnation defeat Christians, because of their failure to move a mountain. They hear many people relate how their mountain just "got right up" and moved away. They were healed, loved ones were saved, finances came in! But this desperate individual, who has tried so hard, is still battling his same problems.

After hearing so many of these stories, I feel like saying, "Forget the mountain and begin to use your mouth and your heart to draw near to God." As someone so ably put it, "God's faith is so high and mine is so low, I just trust the grace of God to make up the difference." Bask in His presence, worship at His feet. If you have to take medicine or borrow money, praise Him even more! What does moving a mountain have to do with your relationship with Jesus? Nothing!! Before you know it, you will be a first class mountain mover. You won't really know just when you first started, and by now you have moved so many you have forgotten to count them! Maybe God doesn't want us *counting our blessings* as much as He wants us *enjoying the Blesser!*

The next time you can't move a mountain . . . climb on top of it and shout your praises, as Israel did to the walls of Jericho; and watch that mountain crumble and tumble down. Then next time you are prayed for, and the symptoms remain, say, "That's all right, symptoms — even if I have to go to the hospital, Jesus is still my Lord, and I will accept no condemnation!"

Teaching faith principles must include II Corinthians 4:13. "We having the same spirit of faith, according as it is written, I believed, and therefore have I spoken; we also believe, and therefore speak." The spirit of faith resided in the Old Testament saints because this passage was first written in Psalms 116:10a. The 11th chapter of Hebrews gives a vivid account of some of these miracles beginning with Abel and ending by saying that "God, having provided some better thing for us, that they without us should not be made perfect."

We are to receive more than they had . . . do even greater works than they or Jesus did. John 14:12 says, "Verily, verily, I say unto you, He that believeth on me, the works that I do shall he do also; and greater works than these shall he do; because I go unto my Father." They had a spirit of faith. It was deeply imbedded in them. I can almost hear them, rising early in the morning, and singing, "Hear, O Israel, the Lord our God is mighty, He is our salvation." Most of us in America arise to a cup of coffee and the morning news. They began their day with worship. We, in the 20th century, begin ours with worry. The spirit of faith is constantly speaking God's Word, constantly affirming what is written. One of the greatest principles of faith as taught in the Word is the heart (spirit) of man believing what is written and the mouth (soul) of man in perfect agreement by saying it.

Elsewhere we shall speak concerning the building up of the spirit in order to believe more easily.

Very few teachers of the Word have noticed the continuity of the faith principle in Mark 11:23 and the next verse, 24, about prayer. These verses, one on faith and the other on prayer, are tied together by the word, "therefore." The Greek better relates it as "because of that thing." Berry translates it as, "for this reason;" literally meaning, "because of mountain moving faith that just moved my mountain, I am now ready to pray."

God does not instruct us to pray for Him to move the mountain. If the mountain is in the way, *you* are to move it — not God. Next time you have a prayer request, be sure there is not a mountain in the way. Be sure there are no obstacles hindering. God is not promising the answer to the prayer in Verse 24, "whatsoever things ye desire," until Verse 23 is complied with. What you want God to do follows what you are to do.

A good example of this will be a great desire in the heart of a husband or wife to have a better marriage relationship. They are praying but nothing is happening. There are some mountains, barriers, hindrances in the way. They are not doing anything about it . . . just praying for things to get better between them. Sometimes the mountain is an unforgiving spirit over something that one of them did, even before they were married. Sometimes it is just a personality difference because of the differences in background and culture. The mountain that separates them is movable — so move it!

Roy Hicks, Jr., pastor of Faith Center in Eugene, Oregon, preaches a sermon on mountain moving faith from Zechariah 4:7, "Who art thou, O great mountain? Before Zerubbabel thou shalt become a plain: and he shall bring forth the headstone thereof with shoutings, crying, Grace, grace unto it," and Micah 6:1b, "Arise, contend thou before the mountains, and let the hills hear thy voice." Speaking grace, singing grace, shouting grace . . . contending, raising your voice . . . God's Word declares if you do it, the mountain will move and where that mountain was, there will be a plain! Grace is the unmerited favor of God. Grace is the power of God that brought Jesus to us. For by grace (God's ability and power) are ye saved. It is by this same grace that the mountain will move. Take authority against that problem. Do all you can do. Then, whatsoever ye desire when ye pray, believe. Believe that you have it and it shall be yours.

Faith principles are unchangeable. They will work. Move that mountain . . . then enter into prayer for your desires.

A little boy built a bird trap. His young sister told her mother that she was going to pray that it wouldn't work. The mother noticed that she was praying with a great amount of confidence and assurance. When she asked her daughter how she could pray with so much faith, she answered, "I just went out and kicked down the bird trap!" What she really did, in effect, was to move her mountain before she prayed.

The Lord, by His Spirit, ministered a beautiful truth to one congregation. The Spirit called attention to the fact that so many times our prayers are about things of the past. Nothing can be done about many of these things now, because it is simply too late. Jesus usually addressed Himself (in prayer) to things of the future. Note His prayer in the garden as He faced the cross, His prayer in John 17, His prayer at Lazarus' tomb. This is good counsel of the Holy Spirit. If we will move our mountains, by the agreeing of our mouth with our heart by speaking grace, contending against it, then our praying can be directed toward the future. Our spiritual relationship will mature more easily.

It was the author's privilege recently to lead a large congregation of hundreds of voices to shout "grace" to the weather pattern. A large high pressure system had settled in and was causing prolonged unusual weather. The weather forecasters predicted the pattern was to remain. That very night the high pressure system began to weaken; the weather changed and much needed rain began to fall on the West Coast.

Arise, contend thou before the mountain! Speak grace to your mountain. Believe God's words. If you do, you will act accordingly.

Do not ignore faith principles; let them work for you. Always remember, faith never struggles . . . it rests.

4

Principle Not Formula

In the two preceding chapters I spoke about the great principles of prayer and faith. These two great principles form the foundation of the Christian warfare. Without prayer and faith we would have no spiritual weapons, either for defense or offense. One of the greatest causes of failure of prayer or faith's confession of the Word is the confusion of the great principles of prayer and faith with that of mere formula. Instead of being principle, they are only formula.

The author has been in error in many of his past sermons by misuse of the word "formula." One day I took the time to look it up in Webster's Dictionary. It defines it in its two primary meanings as, "A fixed form of words, especially one that has lost its original meaning or force and is now used only as a conversational or ceremonial expression or repeated without thought." One can readily see what we are referring to when we say failures come as a result of principle becoming formula. How so many of our religious cliches have started as principles, but have degenerated into formulas! Some will even be heard to say, lightly and in jest, "Don't say that, you will have whatever you say!" While it is true that this is a great cardinal precious truth, just half of it (saying it—especially in jest) won't work. The faith principle is to *believe* what you say.

Many have gone to hear a great faith teacher speak on the subject of confession of the Word and they have heard it presented very positively. They lack depth and somehow miss the crux of the message and go away attempting to apply only that part of the message they wanted to hear, by saying things like, "I will become a millionaire . . . I will become a millionaire." Or, "I will drive a Cadillac . . . I will drive a Cadillac . . ." or, "I will get a better job . . ." etc. So many, who in life style are fair weather Christians, wait until they are in deep trouble, then get very religious in order to get themselves out. They will try anything — religious formulas, cliches, spiritual jargon — grasping at every straw. As Richard P. Cook said, "Most of us have much trouble praying when we are in little trouble, but we have little trouble praying when we are in much trouble."

The fixed formulas of science such as are in medicine and mathematics will always work because you cannot tamper with them. Two and two are four and always will be. But to attempt, "Our Father, who art in heaven . . ." *without relationship with Him* is to try to reduce the greatest of principles of prayer into a "quickie" formula. It becomes a ceremonial expression and reduces the great principle of prayer and faith's confession to a non-productive expression.

A young man attended a faith seminar and listened to the speaker present a faith message on Mark 11:23, "Ye shall have whatever ye say . . ." The young man's wife had left him . . . and, after hearing the great principle of faith taught, he went away repeating over and over literally hundreds of times, "My wife will come back to me, my wife will come back to me." But she didn't. She married someone else. Faith preachers and teachers must be positive; at the same time they should be honest. If a listener is misguided, the teacher must assume some responsibility.

Similar incidents are common. Elsewhere I talked about folk only turning to God in a crisis. They really do not want a relationship with Jesus . . . just an answer to their prayers. Faith teachers and pastors should be cognizant of this problem. As able ministers of the Word we should strive to present the whole truth in such a way that it ministers help to the seeker rather than just making the speaker appear great and be the recipient of much adulation. Many, many seekers are not ready to write their own tickets with God. They do not even know the "conductor" yet. There is no need to excite faith with fantastic illustration. Excited faith only steps out of the boat and goes under. But there is a need to present Jesus as Lord and lead people to a beautiful relationship with Him.

Perhaps some pastors and faith teachers are afraid to reveal some of the frustrations experienced by unanswered prayer. They may fear this will only weaken the message. Jesus didn't seem to have this fear. He always told the truth, the whole truth, and nothing but the truth. The Bible even records the greatest failure of all. Satan, God's choice angel . . . Judas Iscariot's betrayal of Jesus . . . and Peter's denial. Jesus taught that not all of the seed sown will reap a hundredfold. Some will reap sixty and others only thirty.

Some people come to a divine healing meeting for the healing of their physical bodies only. Their real need is Jesus. I have always admired Kenneth Hagin's ministry because he never fails to give an altar call for salvation first. That is his priority! The goal of faith teachers should be found in the balance of teaching and ministering to the whole man, not just a part of him. Reach him on the level of his intelligence and spiritual age rather than from the level and spiritual experience of the speaker. Many religions of the world work by formula. Adam Clark mentions how so many of the Mohammedan's prayers are formed of just one or two words repeated over and over

again. Jesus' admonition not to use the repetitive phraseology was against mere religious formula.

Some religions work through magic — with the casting of spells or hexes against their enemies; piercing with
pins little images of the ones they want to afflict. They
mix deadly potions, all done by formulas that are passed
down from generation to generation. Some of them work
some of the time. Most of them fail most of the time.

Many Christians are always on the lookout for formulas. They want to take the short cut, the magic wand,
if they can find it. We are even programmed to react to
certain cliches that come from the platform. If the service
begins to lag, then the speaker will begin to use his
formulas to work up the people. The people have been
programmed to respond with the right thing at the right
time . . . and will help the speaker to get the service
moving again. (This is especially true if the speaker neglected to pray and prepare as he should.)

Probably what is known in Pentecostal circles as the
"Jericho march" is a good example of a principle which
has now become a formula. The initial Jericho march
could have been in the inspiration and anointing of the
Holy Spirit. Others tried it because they heard about it.
Perhaps the first time they did it there was a measure of
blessing in it because it was a new thing — but by the
third or fourth time a principle had become a formula.
We have been in a part of the nation where a "prayer
chair" is used. Individuals who are to be prayed for must
sit in that particular chair in order to be healed . . . even
to the point of requiring a sick person to get out of bed
to sit in the "chair" before they can pray.

The author recalls a certain evangelist who had con-
ducted many city-wide meetings in which all of the
pentecostal churches cooperated. The evangelist remarked
that he could pick out the different groups by their reac-

tion to the moving of the Spirit of the Lord. Some groups were programmed to jerk, some to shake, some to run, and some to fall on the floor. Is there anything wrong with shaking, jerking, running, or falling? No. A thousand times no. They were simply responding to the characteristic reactions of their particular group as the Spirit of God moved upon them. It is a thousand times wrong if they have taken something that was genuine at the beginning and have now reduced it to a meaningless formula.

One evangelist even boasts about his ability to get people to fall when he prays for them. He said, in his words, "I stand real close and push gently but firmly on their heads." A good formula for him to reap his desired end . . . but wrong in principle. The author has seen people fall as a result of the real power of God, and when this happens there is no need of an "assist" from the evangelist. There is the real . . . and the counterfeit. But we will never sacrifice the principles just because someone has reduced them to formula. Anointing with oil is a great principle in the Bible. No doubt it has also been used as a formula. Communion, the remembering of the life and death and resurrection of our Lord, is a blessed time. It is a God-given principle. The next time you are privileged to receive the sacraments, try to analyze and see if you are receiving in Spirit . . . or only going through the motions, hoping it will soon be over so you can be on your way, thus reducing one of God's greatest principles to mere formula.

Many of our own evangelical forms of worship have been reduced to formulas. The song service, the time of the service when we open the hymn books, can be a great and inspired time to encourage worship. This is a principle. But, the constant habitual singing of the same few hymns over and over again will soon reduce the beautiful principle to mere formula . . . one that has lost its meaning through repetitive usage. We stand to pray, take prayer requests, and someone is asked to lead in prayer. This great principle is reduced to mere formula in many churches by the monotony of the same people being chosen to lead in prayer in every service, mainly because they have an ability with words — pleasant to hear but powerless to move! Real prayer is head and heart conversation with God. A few prayers prayed from the head and heart in every church next Sunday night might stir a few folks enough to at least know God might just be listening! Some churches are "air-conditioned" — and what we really need are some "prayer-conditioned" ones.

Faith confession and the power of prayer are great principles. They are given to us by the Holy Spirit of God. The world itself could not hold the books if all the results of answered prayers were recorded. These great God-given principles work. Failure cannot erase them. Time cannot erode them. The abuse by reducing them to formulas may try to weaken them but can never kill them. They are eternal . . . forever settled in heaven. Do not be afraid to stand on them, to use them, to propagate them. They work. Principles will *work for you* . . . but *you work* formulas. Pray and confess your faith. You are on the right track, don't fall into the formula rut. The next time you are praying for something, be sure to check your relationship with the Lord Jesus. Principles can easily be reduced to formulas if the relationship is weak. The Lord, in a word of prophecy, spoke and said, "I will not answer prayer just to protect my reputation." Principles must be acted upon, believed. Formulas only produce frustrations.

5

Telling God's Secrets

Joshua 6:10:

And Joshua had commanded the people, saying, Ye shall not shout, nor make any noise with your voice, neither shall any word proceed out of your mouth, until the day I bid you shout; then shall ye shout.

Matthew 8:4a

See thou tell no man.

Matthew 9:30b

See that no man know it.

Matthew 16:20

Then charged he his disciples that they should tell no man that he was Jesus the Christ. (And Matthew 12:16)

Matthew 17:9b

Tell the vision to no man, until the Son of Man be risen again from the dead. (Mark 3:12)

Mark 5:43

. . . that no man should know it. (Mark 7:36)

Mark 8:26

And he sent him away to his house, saying, Neither go into the town, nor tell it to any in the town.

Luke 8:56

And her parents were astonished: but he charged them that they should tell no man what was done.

Deuteronomy 29:29

The secret things belong unto the Lord our God: but those things which are revealed (released) belong unto us and to our children for ever, that we may do all the words of this law.

Mark 5:19

Go home to thy friends, and tell them how great things the Lord hath done for thee.

One of the areas of misunderstanding and difficulty is when to keep something to yourself and when to tell it. Ecclesiastes 3:7b declares there is "A time to keep silence, and a time to speak."

We, as a church, have never been taught that there are cruical times in God's Kingdom when one is to keep silence. We have always been directed to go our way and tell what God has done for us, but we have never suggested that telling it indiscriminately can also be a good way to lose it. The church, especially Pentecostals, have been notorious about putting people in front of others to tell what God has done for them. This has often been done with an implied warning that if you do not, you will lose the healing or deliverance. Never, but never, in the history of the church, have we been taught what is taught in Scripture. We have always assumed, because Jesus told some people to go and show what great things God has done for them, that He meant that they always should tell everything that God has done. Did He ever tell people to go their way and keep quiet? Yes, *far more often*. He asked people to cooperate with Him by being quiet. By being quiet, they were helping Him, cooperating with Him, by going and telling it, they were hindering Him, and in some cases making it impossible for Him to continue to work in that place.

Some psychologists have dared to suggest that what Jesus was really doing was using reverse psychology. He actually wanted them to go and tell it; not really keep quiet. But neither the Scriptures nor what followed supports this.

Some people, by telling about their healing, lost it immediately. While speaking recently, the author was suggesting that we could lose our healing by telling it; a man was present who, just that past week, had that experience. He was healed in a divine healing campaign and he related how God had healed him — and he lost the healing that very day. The author is not suggesting that we refrain from giving praise to God for our healing, nor am I suggesting that you never tell it. What I am suggesting is that we try to understand if there should be times when it is in the best interest of all concerned that we keep silence.

Let us examine some reasons why it may be best not to share our victory.

First, *timing* is very important in all things. Just to go and promiscuously or at random tell it would possibly only raise questions and trigger doubt. As an illustration: to stand up on Sunday morning in a church service when the flu is going around and tell how you were awakened during the night by all the flu symptoms, you prayed and they left immediately, will not be a great blessing to a host of people who woke up and threw up. Now, it meant a great deal to you. You believe that God healed you. Most of them believe it was not even the flu, but probably indigestion, or something far inferior to what they had. Why not permit yourself to sit there and enjoy that great blessing of the night before, rather than to cast out your lonely pearl, only to have it trampled on. Perhaps there will be a better time to relate the testimony. At least you ought to have asked God if you should have told it or not. Timing is also very important concerning financial blessing. To be unwise in relating what God did for you in a great area of poverty can cause deep resentment against you and against God.

Secondly, a great reason not to tell a thing until God wants you to is that it makes God look as though He is a respecter of person. Can you hear God say: "I would love to do that for you. I know you have faith, but if I do that, you will go and tell it and cause five little ones to resent me." Of course I cannot prove this by illustrations in the Bible, but we do know that He did ask a lot of people to keep a secret with Him.

A third reason why we should not tell it is because we have a tendency to make man look greater than God. For instance, in the real life situation I related earlier about the man who lost his healing by telling it, he was asked by his pastor to come forward and tell it. (Pastors need this chapter also.) The evangelist who had prayed for him was put in a great light. Immediately many people said, "My, what a great person that man must be. If he ever comes here again I will have him pray for me." God has, of necessity, many times allowed great humbling things happen to people to whom He had given gifts, because we are prone to exalt the individual and make them look even mightier than God, who actually did the miracle. Perhaps it could release God to heal more people if He could trust us to keep His secrets.

Here is a fourth reason why we would be better off at times not to share it. Many people cannot tell a thing without making the "I" look better than the "I" should look. In fact, when they get through telling it, it looks like this: " 'I' want to thank God that He healed 'ME'. 'I' was sick and 'I' believed God and 'I' received 'MY' healing: Now if you will be like 'ME' you, too, can be healed."

Maybe this is a little exaggerated, but all of us have discerned some pretty big "I's" in the testimony.

A fifth reason why some should not tell it, is because they received their healing on somebody else's faith. God honored that ministry. God is compassionate, gracious, and is more desirous to do than sometimes we are to receive. His very nature is goodness. But a person, having received because of somebody else's faith, was not ready to take on the devil. Then he began to declare it about, the enemy took a crack at him, and because of his lack of knowledge of how to resist the devil, he wavered and was uncertain when the symptoms returned. The author knows of one person whose healing was confirmed by the doctors, yet the sickness returned, and he died. In this particular situation, the story was shared abroad, loud and long, and many were talking about it.

To ask God whether or not one should tell his victory makes great sense to me. After all, He was the one who gave the victory, or answered the prayer — should not He also be the one I should look to as whether or not I should tell it, or at least, *when* I should tell it? The wise man said, "a time to keep quiet and a time to speak," good advice was given to all.

In Matthew 5:37, our Lord asks us to let our communication be yea and nay and "whatsoever is more than these cometh (causeth) of evil." How many times we have counselled the new born-again baby to go back to work and call everybody around and tell them how he got saved. Bad advice. Not only from a testimonial standpoint, but would it not look pretty stupid to place a new baby, only a few days old, before a big crowd and say: "Now tell how you were born." The infant would be capable of some cooing and crying, but it would not be ready to answer any questions as to how it happened to be born. Would not it be best for those new Christians to grow in the grace of God, mature, and get some answers before they are instructed to go and tell their story? Notice that Jesus asked the disciples not to talk about the transfiguration. The others were not ready for it. Can you hear the rest of the disciples asking: "Why didn't the Lord take us along? What did Moses and Elias have to say? How did they look? How do you know it was them? Maybe it was an angel!" It is not hard to figure out why the Lord asked them to keep quiet.

Now He did tell the man, out of whom he had cast the demons, to go and tell the great thing God had done for him. This is easy to understand. Had this demoniac attempted to return again, the men of the city would have attacked him. They would not have allowed that crazy man back into town. But you can see him put up his hands and say: "Wait a minute, fellows, I am not the same man. Jesus of Nazareth has healed me. Legion is gone. I am all right." It was the wisdom of the Lord, in this case, to tell the man to go and tell what great things the Lord had done for him.

Another example of how we miss it in not seeking the wisdom of God is in a situation that can develop during prayer time. Many requests are made at this time. Much pressure is applied by the leader to have the people make their requests known. Sometimes it seems as though the leader has somehow failed if no one raises a hand to tell of a need! Enough so that, if no one raises a hand, sometimes a little pressure is applied . . . and people search around in their minds to see if they can't find a request! If you have ever experienced one of these times, you have no doubt heard even ridiculous requests. Someone asked prayer for a neighbor with a broken leg. Now, I would not know how to pray for this neighbor with a broken leg. Do I need to pray for his soul? Do I need to pray for his healing . . . or does he need to have the other leg broken?! When making prayer requests, remember to give direction.

God expects us to be business-like in prayer, as well as in business. During many of our prayer request times we have had desperate situations brought to our attention. The author, being a pastor for many years, has experienced many of these times. The need is great, urgent. The believers fervently pray and believe as we follow the scripture admonition to pray for one another. After the prayers are prayed, someone will say, "The Lord just witnessed to my heart that the prayer is heard and the answer is on the way!" Immediately there is mixed reaction. Some will think, "I wonder why the Lord told them and not me?" Others will say, "Praise the Lord for answering." They will then mark that request off and stop believing. The person for whom all the people prayed fails to receive the answer for the request, and their faith is shaken.

If you ever find yourself fortunate enough for the Lord to bear witness with you about what He is doing . . . keep silence. Do not speak it aloud. God's Word is very specific about the fact that He always bears witness on the earth. "In the mouth of two or three witnesses let every word be established." When God was going to destroy the cities of Sodom and Gommorrah, He witnessed with Abraham His intent . . . but Abraham did not send runners into the cities to tell them what God was going to do.

Let us keep God's secrets. Let us become trustworthy and sensitive. The next time God does something great for you or your prayer was answered, why not ask Him if you should tell it? At least ask Him *when* you should tell it. Maybe, just maybe, before Jesus comes back we will learn a few things we should have known all along. It is taught in the Word. Let us, by the help of the Holy Spirit, learn why . . . and learn how to cooperate with God.

6

The Curse of Time

In my book on laughter there is a chapter that talks about God sitting in the "hub" of eternity. He lives in timelessness and deals with us who are in the time dimension. Lack of understanding of this great truth causes many to lose faith in God. It is often very difficult for us to understand how God can have time to be able to hear and deal with (personally) literally thousands of people all praying at the same time. The difficulty arises because we are unable to believe confidently that He is hearing us and really listening to us!

Oh that we could understand that God is never affected by either numbers or time. He created us, all of us, millions of us. He not only knows all of us, our names, our ages, the number of hairs on our heads — He knows our thoughts and our plans, our past and our future and has a record of all we have ever said and done. In all of this He is not in the least bit confused! He knows us corporately; He also knows us each individually. He loves you and cares very much about you. You see, He has always loved you (Romans 5:8), even when you were a violent sinner. He loved you. Because you received Him as your Lord, He didn't suddenly begin to love you more. In fact, there is nothing you can, or will ever do, to stop His loving you (Romans 8:38, 39). God's *attitude* toward you is one of love. Love will always seek out your good, what is best for you.

You might ask, "Why, then, will people be in hell?" How can God do that to them if He loved them?" This is very easy to understand when you realize that God also hates sin (Proverbs 16:6). He cannot tolerate sin. He, because of His nature of holiness, must deal with and punish sin and all of those who persist in holding on to their sins. He loves the person. He longs for that person to turn from his sin. Sin is to be finally cast into hell, and because sin is in that person, (by either the act or imagination) then he also must, of necessity, be cast into hell.

Many Christians carry resentment against God because of their fear of punishment and even because of their thoughts of being sent to hell. God created you, loves you, and wants you with Him eternally. The element of time can be a blessing or a curse to you. God does not determine that — you do. When I turn to God and receive His son, Jesus, as my Savior, I then begin to cultivate all of the attitudes I find in God. They are not my attitudes by nature. I must introduce them and begin to indoctrinate my soulish realm.

This takes time . . . time that will allow me to mature. I need this time. It is not initially an enemy, but if I am not careful, I will let it become so. Most of us are very impatient and feel we are not growing, but God, our Father, living in timelessness, looks back and sees how far we have come. He also sees where we are going and rejoices in our progress. A parent, praying for his son or daughter during the difficult teenage years, may often become discouraged becauses he only sees the heartache of the present. God, because He sits in eternity and sees also the future, can see the fruit of that father's prayer for his child. He sees the child turning to Jesus and beginning a new life, free from all of the past. We do not have this overview and so cannot be blessed by it as God is. But let us at least comprehend that much of our eternal Father's omniscience.

Now let us deal with that aspect of prayer and its "hoped for" answer within the scope of the time dimension, which sometimes becomes our enemy. To illustrate this, let us say a father is playing a game with his son. Naturally it is easy to beat the son in competition because of the experience and ability of the father. The father may say, "Give that boy a few years and he will be able to beat me easily." But, at the same time, the child may go away very frustrated saying, "I'll never try again." I wonder how many times we have engaged in a spiritual contest, lost, and gave up. If we could have heard the Heavenly Father's words in the other dimension, we might have heard, "Give that saint just a little more time in the Word and in worship and the devil better look out! Angels! Prepare some answers, that saint will be back and when he comes he will be ready to abundantly receive."

Let us assume I visit you in the hospital. You have asked God to heal you and yet you need an operation. Because it was of a very serious nature, one you could not postpone, such as an emergency appendectomy, you didn't have time to seek God or wait upon Him. The attack had caught you very much unprepared. This would be an excuse; and shame on you for having neglected your relationship with God! But it was just one of those things. Given a little time perhaps you could have handled that sickness. However, the operation was urgent and you did not have the time factor in your favor. What do you do now? First, do not allow the enemy to condemn you. *Whether or not you are successful in appropriating every time in every instance . . . has nothing to do with your relationship with your Father.* His love is not based on whether or not you have an operation. He still loves you, has always loved you, and will always love you. Take it from there. Continue to worship and quote Romans 8:1a, "There is no doom now for those who are in Christ." (Mof.) It is not the end of the world! Romans 8:28, "We know also that those who love God have His aid and interest in everything . . ." (Mof). Williams translated it, "Yes, we know that all things go on working together for the good of those who keep on loving God."

Just keep on loving God. The insufficiency of time that was against you when you needed an immediate operation or when you had to borrow money quickly can now work for you. But you must make it work. It will not naturally work for you. Time will work against you if you permit it to do so. Snatch a few minutes, be alone with God — and be in the Word. If you will make time work *for* you, then time can never be *against* you. You are always ready for it, or any emergency that arises.

Another instance when time will work against you is when you are ruled more by a quick emotional release than a release of faith. Have you ever been in a religious service where the speaker is doing a good professional job of presenting his case, and the excitement and fervour are running high? Great promises are quoted and they are good. Then the pitch, "Everyone who believes in God, get out the biggest bill in your wallet or purse. Bring it up and I will pray a special prayer for your healing." You do believe in God. You do need healing. So you respond. You did not receive healing (it is not a commodity that can be purchased). You did not get a return for your money . . . because you gave in emotion, not faith. A few days go by. You have had time to think and now wish you had not done it. Of course God looked ahead and saw your disappointment — even before you gave the offering.

Now what lesson can we learn from this? Time, the *lack* of it, did not permit you to make a sound decision. The next time you feel that kind of pressure, say to yourself, "Lord, if I am to give this man $100.00, speak to me and keep on speaking. If I feel this same way 30 minutes from now, or 3 days from now, I will give it to him." If the cause has merit, you can give in faith rather than emotion that later on turns into doubt. Many pastors have had to "pick up the pieces" among their frustrated sheep because of this kind of "time pressure" tactic.

Another way time can work against you is in your extreme and great desire to grow in the grace and knowledge of God. You hear speakers of great ability and force, such as the Kenneth Hagins, the Billy Grahams, and the Jack Hayfords, and you covet that kind of relationship with God. You have been at it for all of three months, and you are already wanting to give up. How long do you think it took great men to achieve this kind of maturity? It was not overnight. God would enjoy seeing all of His children grow up overnight — but, you know what? If God did everything for us, none of us could appreciate it.

Have you ever observed a small child that we would term a "spoiled brat?" How did he get that way? His parents indulged him in his every desire and whim all the time and every occasion. Many things that should have been denied him until he reached an age of maturity, enough to value them, were bestowed. Another boy down the street worked and earned enough to buy a car. The parents of the aforementioned boy bought one for him. He promptly took it out and, in one trip, burned out the motor. But he is not concerned, his parents will buy him another one. Will he ever appreciate what is given him in an effort to indulge and pamper him? No! Because he has never been allowed time to develop and learn for himself. Someone was always doing *for* him.

God has allowed us time, as a gift, in order to grow and mature in Him. Take that time, all you need, to read, study, pray and worship. Learn to love, to weep, to rejoice. Put your shoulder to the gospel wheel and push. This kind of exercise will cause you to develop and grow quickly and as rapidly as possible. All that God needs to see is not where you are, but where you are heading. You are determined not to stay where you are . . . so you are asking, seeking and knocking. When God can look ahead and see your goals then He will be able to cross your pathway with excellent teachers and pastors, and they will all help you reach that goal. In fact, God will overlook tremendous weaknesses where you are now, if He can look ahead and see that your determination to move forward will not waver. He can even bless you with some "goodies" (present tense) that others cannot receive because they are standing still. Time is working for you, and so is your Father, who is saying, "Keep that up, my child . . . all of the angels of heaven are pulling for you." Make time work for you and it will not work against you.

7

Casting Down Imaginations

Imaginations are not always funny. Years ago there was a popular song that said, "Imagination is funny . . . it makes the cloudy day sunny." This may be true if you are not having a problem. But it can also turn the sunny day cloudy, by the mere flip of the imagination. II Corinthians 10:5 says, "Casting down imaginations (reasonings), and every high thing that exalteth itself against the knowledge of God, and bringing into captivity every thought to the obedience of Christ." Here we have great, but overlooked, teaching that will help us in our prayer life.

The imagination — that part of the mind that can form a picture without ever seeing it, that part of the mind that can make a picture better or worse than the reality, that part of the mind that constantly brings before us all our past failures and clouds the hopes of the future. That part of the mind can be a very great asset to your faith and prayers . . . or a very great hindrance.

How many times have God's own dear children prayed with faith and confidence and then allowed the enemy to gain control of their imaginations. Instead of seeing a picture of victory, they see a picture of defeat. For instance, when you ask prayer for healing of your body, do you see yourself in the future healthy and happy or do you picture yourself suffering and even having surgery? The author has even heard people say they pictured in their imagination their own funeral. They even saw those who attended and heard their comments as they passed by the casket. Some people, after much prayer over their finances, have pictured new accounts coming their way, or unexpected money in the mail; while others, after praying, have gone their way planning in their imagination just how they will borrow the needed money; seeing their house and car repossessed if they do not obtain help. They are looking for all of the alternatives if God does not come through by answering their prayer.

Psalms 139:1 and 2 says, "O Lord, thou has searched me, and known me. Thou knowest my downsitting and mine uprising, thou understandest my thought afar off." Our thoughts are not hidden from God. He knows what you are thinking, even though your lips may be saying something else.

How do we use our imaginations to work *with* our prayers and not against them? How well do I remember when God answered one of the first prayers I ever prayed to receive a material blessing. I had not been in the ministry very long and I needed a car very badly. I recall making this a matter of prayer. I will have to admit that I didn't know then all that I know now about prayer and faith . . . but I was acting on all I did know. One day, as I was in prayer, suddenly I saw myself, in my imagination, driving down the highway in that very car I was asking the Father to give me. It was so real that, as I prayed, I began to rejoice and be happy. Soon after that the car became mine. As I drove it down the road one day, I wondered why I wasn't experiencing a great feeling of exultation. Then I remembered back to the time when I asked God for the car . . . and had the great sense of thanksgiving and rejoicing. I had already experienced the thrill of ownership in my imagination — and had no need to experience it again!

When the twelve spies were sent in to spy out the land, some of them came back with very negative reports. It is true that they saw giants, walled cities, chariots of iron, etc. What happened when they saw these formidable obstacles? Their imaginations were activated and began to compare themselves against the giants. Naturally they would see themselves pulverized by these big bruisers. When they saw how small they were and how massive and high the walls of the cities were, their imaginations staggered to see how they could ever be able to conquer them. Ten of the spies' imaginations worked against them. Unbelief came in and they came back to Moses defeated. It cost them their lives . . . and cost the people of God being able to enjoy the promised land. Two of the spies, Joshua and Caleb, had seen the same giants and walled cities, but they disciplined their imaginations to work for them, instead of against them. Instead of seeing how big the enemy was, they saw the immensity of God. Read Numbers 13 and 14 for this exciting account. Because he refused to picture defeat, God said of Caleb that he "had another spirit" with him (Numbers 14:24). It takes another spirit to trigger positive imaginations when all seems to be against you. Begin to picture defeat and Satan will take advantage of your weaknesses. Picture victory and God will fortify your weakness and turn it into strength.

David, as a boy just in from the hillside where he had been watching the sheep and singing praises to God, saw Goliath in a much different light than did his brothers who had been looking at his great size and listening to his boastful challenges and listening to the talk among other soldiers. They cringed in fear at his booming, defiant voice. They could see themselves going out to meet his challenge and being run through with his gigantic spear, their heads cut off and being held aloft, while Goliath taunted Israel's armies even more vociferously. David, in his imagination, saw the picture far differently. He saw this giant coming, not against a lad, but against the God of Israel. In his mind no one, but no one, could survive who cursed his God. This giant was "duck soup." In David's imagination he saw the stone sink deep into the forehead of Goliath and saw him topple. He did not see defeat . . . he only saw victory! It is this kind of imagination that works for you, not against you.

Jesus knew and could see Himself killed by the soldiers; he could see Himself being taken from the cross and buried. He also could see something else. What else He saw is recorded in Hebrews 12:2b, "Who for the joy that was set before Him endured the cross." What did He see? He saw Himself seated at the right hand of God, the Father. He could see millions being redeemed from their sins. Encouragement for us in this realm is found in the words of Hebrews 12:3, "For consider Him (Jesus) that endured such contradiction of sinners against himself, lest ye be wearied and faint in *your minds.*"

What do you see when you pray? How far away is heaven? Does Jesus have a smile on His face as you pray . . . or a frown? Are things working for you, or against you? Remember you are in prayer, petitioning the Father and your mind will imagine either positive or negative thoughts and pictures. Hebrew 8:10 speaks of God putting his laws in our minds (imagination). God promised that He would put His promises in our imagination. If we have doubts and fears and wrong pictures of defeat . . . then God's promises are displaced. God wants us to love Him with our imaginations (mind) and hearts. (Matthew 2:37 and repeated again in Mark 12:30 and Luke 10:27.) Each time He uses the Greek work "dianoia." This could be translated "imagination." Vincent and Strong's Concordance both say this means "faculty of thought."

Luke 12:27-29 reads, "Consider the lilies how they grow: they toil not, they spin not; and yet I say unto you, that Solomon in all his glory was not arrayed like one of these. If then God so clothe the grass, which is today in the field, and tomorrow is cast into the oven; how much more will he clothe you, O ye of little faith? And seek not ye what ye shall eat, or what ye shall drink, neither be ye of doubtful mind." All of these promises are followed with the admonition, "do not have a doubtful mind," using the Greek work "dianoia" (imagination). Do not let your mind entertain doubt, fear, and unbelief. In Colossians 1:21 we are alienated and enemies by our imaginations; I Peter 1:13 admonishes us to gird up the loins (source of reproductive power — W. E. Vine) of our mind (imagination). The generating power of our minds can be for good or evil . . . positive or negative.

Spiritual imagination works with your "born again spirit." A doubting, fearful imagination works from the soulish realm and is open to attack and harassment from the enemy. Romans 12:2a says, "Be not conformed to this world (don't let the world squeeze you into its own mold . . . Phillips) but be ye transformed by the renewing of your mind (by its new ideals and its new attitudes . . . Amp.)" Transformation comes by the renewing of the thought patterns of your mind. In the great faith chapter, Hebrews 11, one notices how often the mind and imagination is referred to: "having seen;" "being mindful;" "endured as seeing him who is invisible;" "evidence of things not seen;" "he looked for a city" (one he had not yet seen); "having seen them afar off;" "were persuaded." Prayers of faith must work with the imagination.

Begin to think spiritual thoughts and talk spiritual talk. Your prayer life will be greatly improved as you order control over your imaginations.

Recently the author received a letter from a lady who had attended many faith seminars and had practiced all of the truths she had received. In all of her attempts to say the right thing, quoting the right scriptures, etc., she experienced frustrations and failure. In her words she,

"Never wanted to hear another sermon on faith." It was during this time of discouragement that she attended a service where I was speaking. It was on a night when I ministered on using your imagination in worship. It opened up a whole new dimension for her. She saw herself worshipping at the feet of Jesus. After a few weeks of this beautifully improved relationship, she found it easy to begin to receive from the Lord.

There is a "switch" you can use to turn on the spiritual mind. Do it, use it, and prayers will more easily be prayed . . . and the answers received.

8

When God Can't Hear Me

I John 5:14 and 15, "And this is the confidence (outspokenness . . . Strongs) that we have in Him, that, if we ask anything according to his will, he heareth us: and if we know that he hear us, whatsoever we ask, we know that we have the petitions that we desired of him."

Jesus prayed in John 11:41b, 42, "And Jesus lifted up his eyes, and said, Father, I thank thee that thou hast heard me. (42) And I knew that thou hearest me always: but because of the people which stand by I said it, that they may believe that thou hast sent me."

John 9:31, "Now we know that God heareth not sinners: but if any man be a worshipper of God, and doeth his will, him he heareth."

Psalms 66:18, "If I regard iniquity in my heart, the Lord will not hear me."

The above scriptures underline the importance of the prayer being heard by the Father. Whether or not God even hears a physical sound is unimportant. Some think that He does not. What is important is, does He "hear" (give attention to, heed) my prayer!? Again we can use the analogy of the relationship of the earthly parent to his child. This comparison serves to illustrate prayer very well. The parent can do a reasonably good job of ignoring the child when the child is asking for something that is not going to be granted. Children soon learn that one of the reasons a parent will not hear (give heed to) them is because of disobedience. Rather than having the parent acceding to their request, they would probably hear them say, "You would dare ask me for that after the way you have acted!?" The surprise of the people whose answers to prayer did not come . . . is equalled only by the surprise of the Father over the fact that they would dare to presume to come! The relationship hasn't been good. The child knows this and sometimes prefaces the request by saying, "You probably won't let me go, but I'll ask anyway . . ." etc.

The Bible says, If I regard iniquity in my heart, the Lord will not hear me. The first meaning of the Hebrew word "aven" (iniquity) means to exert one's self in vain. It is the picture of a man always running around, out of breath, accomplishing nothing. Not only is he unrighteous and false, he is not doing a very good job at anything he attempts. Now, this man tries to pray . . . to turn to God. Yet in his heart he knows the relationship is not there. What he must do is simple. Get his heart right with God — repent; turn around and face the other way. God does not expect him to become perfect overnight, but He does expect him to settle down spiritually, quit running in circles and become serious about his spiritual life. Quoted at the beginning of this chapter, John 9:31 adds this thought. His need is to begin to worship God . . . to become a worshipper, directly opposed to the iniquity he has been regarding in his heart.

Regarding iniquity in the heart suggests that the pray-er is aware of the disobedience or sin. He is conscious of the wrong doing. You might think, "Why should anyone approach God, knowing he is in the wrong?" You see, people try prayer. They try God. They try being religious. They will try anything but repentance and worship and obedience. It is like a shot in the dark. I have heard people say, "I know I'm not where I ought to be with God, but will you pray for me?" Or, "I know I am a sinner, but maybe God will have mercy upon me." They are not suggesting that they think God will have mercy on them because of any repentance in their hearts, or that they are going to turn away from their sin and wrong doing. If one can use his imagination, he can picture the prayer from this pray-er not rising any higher than the top of his head. Literally, God could say, "I see your mouth moving, but I can't hear a word you say."

The opposite is the person who is asking in the will of God and in confidence. He is heard . . . and is believing for his answer. This, then brings up the biggest of all questions. The question: When is it wrong to ask twice? Both Smith Wigglesworth and Andrew Murray mention the fact that to ask twice is unnecessary and could even be unbelief. There are some who have carried this to the extreme. Others do not believe it is wrong at all to pray and keep on praying . . . which, if kept up continuously, could become repetitious prayer as mentioned in Matthew 6:7a, "But when ye pray, use not vain repetitions." Kenneth Hagin and the author both have had experiences where the pray-er asked twice (or continued to request prayer) for individuals after the prayer was heard . . . and in those instances the persons died.

Inasmuch as we do not have a definite scripture stating this as a doctrine no one can be dogmatic. The scriptures used by most people to teach continuous asking are taken from context . . . such as the instance of the importune man who went to his neighbor for bread and the widow who harassed the unjust judge. Never, but never, compare our heavenly Father to an unjust judge or a reluctant neighbor who would grant a request merely to get rid of someone.

Luke 11:13b, "How much more shall your heavenly Father give . . .". God is a giving Father to those who ask — not to those who batter down the door and make the neighbors angry. Luke 18:7 says, "And shall not God avenge his own elect, which cry day and night unto him, though he bear long with them?" The word avenge is used. The people, because of sin, were in bondage and wanted vengeance . . . not a simple answer to prayer. It may not be needful to pursue and study the complications of the controversial problem of asking twice; perhaps not enough is served by debating it. Enough to say, believe what you will and do not confuse others with your conclusions.

There are some things that we will always make a matter of continuing prayer . . . i.e., those in authority over us, the success of the gospel work and workers, your own spiritual growth. You ask and seek and keep on asking and seeking; you knock and knock, and keep on knocking. This is continuous striving and seeking for the things of God, not for specifics. But in our own need for deliverance and frustrations know this: all you have to do is ask for what you desire and, if it is in God's will, you ALREADY have it.

Again, a good thing to draw from the comparison of a father with his children is this: If a father says to his child, "Yes, I will take you to the park," he means he has given his consent and they will go. If the child comes to his father, and keeps coming time after time, wearying him with repeated questions about "are we going?" and "When are we going?", it is conceivable that the father will soon say, "I said I would take you, now if you ask me one more time, we won't go at all!" God's word is good enough. He said it and He will do it.

Notice, in I John 5:14, the emphasis is on God's will. If a thing is asked "in His will," He hears us. So, if it is not in His will, He will *not hear* us. To determine His will may require much prayer and seeking God . . . especially in the places where the Bible is not specific. The truth of the matter is that there is very little omitted concerning

His will for our lives. We know God's attitude and will toward many things, such as our finances, our health and our families. You do not have to seek God's will on these things. III John 2 says, "Beloved, I wish above all things that thou mayest prosper (materially and continually, W. E. Vine) and be in health, (safe, sound, whole) even as thy soul prospereth." We know God's attitude and will toward your loved one's salvation. Acts 16:31 says, "Believe on the Lord Jesus Christ and thou shalt be saved and thy house (oikes — family, more or less related . . . Strongs)." Jeremiah 31:16, 17 is, "Thus saith the Lord, Refrain thy voice from weeping, and thine eyes from tears: for thy work shall be rewarded, saith the Lord; and they shall come again from the land of the enemy. And there is hope in thine end, saith the Lord, that thy children shall come again to their own border."

We know God's will and attitude toward everything that pertains to our peace and well being. I Timothy 2:2 says it is simply to lead always a life of peace. Most of the frustrated people with whom I talk are usually confused by not knowing God's direction for their lives. They think they are missing God's will. Many believe they should be in full time gospel work, etc. Let these following verses establish your direction and stop worrying. Psalms 37:23, "The steps of a good man are ordered by the Lord: and he delighted in his way." Proverbs 3:5 and 6 also teaches this great truth. Perhaps all frustrations will be taken care of when we come into understanding of God's will and attitude toward righteous people. Remember, the greatest truth that the book of Job teaches is that when God declares a man to be righteous, he is righteous indeed! No one can contest it. God declares us to be righteous in Christ. II Corinthians 5:21, "For he hath made him to be sin for us, who knew no sin; that we might be made the righteousness of God in Him." We do not become righteous by anything we do, except to believe on and receive Jesus Christ as our Savior. When you claim that righteousness, it is God's attitude toward you . . . it is His will. No longer do you have to seek it, just believe and claim and stand firm.

Psalms 34:15 says, "The eyes of the Lord are upon the righteous, and his ears are open unto their cry." Verse 17, "The righteous cry and the Lord heareth, and delivereth them out of all their troubles (not part, all)." Verse 19, "Many are the afflictions of the righteous: but the Lord delivereth him out of them all (not some, all)."

Psalms 37:16, "A little that a righteous man hath is better than the riches of many wicked."

Proverbs 10:22, "The blessing of the Lord is on the head of the righteous; it maketh rich, and to it no sorrow of heart shall be joined." (Sept.)

Proverbs 11:8, "The righteous from distress is drawn out, and the wicked goeth in instead of him." (YLT)

Proverbs 18:10, "The name of the Lord is a strong tower: the righteous runneth into it, and is safe (cannot be touched — Ber)."

The limitations of the size of this book prevents us from going on to make mention of the literally thousands of promises to those who ask according to God's will . . . who *act* according to His will. Not doing His will, or praying in His will, brings confusion to God's purposes and will for His children. Faith's confession for things, prayer for things, remains unanswered because prayer is not being heard (heeded).

I have heard Aimee Semple McPherson relate how she approached the Lord in her usual preparation for the message. She prayed . . . but the Lord had His back turned to her. She said, "Oh, Lord, what is wrong? You are not answering me." The Lord replied, "Do you remember what you said about a certain lady?" Then Mrs. McPherson remembered how she had made a negative remark about this sister in Christ. As she began to repent, the Lord then began to give her the message for that night. It was to be on the 3rd chapter of James about the unruly tongue!

A beautiful, Spirit-filled couple came to me recently. They were experiencing frustrations because of a failure to get an answer to a prayer. It seems their truck had broken down during a trip. They sat by the side of the road, fervently praying that God would cause their truck to start. They sat there believing, waiting, expecting to hear the motor roar into life at any moment. But it didn't happen and they ended up having to call for the tow truck. Their question to me was, "Why didn't God answer?" My immediate response was, "I am glad He didn't." To their surprised "Why?" I replied, "If God answered that prayer, what would your next prayer be? You would be tempted then to ask God to put gas in your tank and retread your tires." I went on to explain that if God answered our every prayer, every time in all circumstances . . . we would soon find that we had lost all self-reliance. God gave us facilities and abilities to be able to meet life's situations. It would be a violation of this law of "self reliance" for Him to intervene in answer to our every prayer. We know that there are times of desperation when there is no way out. God does intervene and answer prayer in those situations. But to have God perform at our every command would soon make God the actor . . . and us the director.

9

Unity Of The Trinity

Matthew 28:19 says, "Go ye therefore, and teach all nations, baptizing them in the name of the Father, and of the Son, and of the Holy Ghost." John 15:26a says, "But when the Comforter (Holy Spirit) is come, whom I (Jesus) will send unto you from the Father . . ." I Thessalonians 5:23 says, "And the very God of peace sanctify you wholly; and I pray God your whole spirit and soul and body be preserved blameless unto the coming of our Lord Jesus Christ."

Just as God is a trinity, three in one, so is the human being. Just as God is tripartite in that He is Father, Son and Holy Spirit . . . so are we as spirit, soul, and body. God's power and authority is released through the unity of His Trinity. Jesus said in John 14:9, "He that hath seen me hath seen the Father." In John 14:10 Jesus relates that the words He spoke and works He did were all from the Father. Jesus came to support the Father. He was in complete submission to Him. "Not my will but thine be done," He prayed. It would have disrupted the whole plan of God had Jesus gone His own way and said His own words. If you were to ask the Father a question, and then would ask the Son and the Holy Spirit the same question, you would receive an answer in total agreement with what the Father had said. Just as Jesus came to support the Father, so the Holy Spirit came to support and share abroad the words of the Lord Jesus. The Holy Spirit always points men to Christ, not to Himself. Pages could be written concerning the unity of God's Trinity, so we will not belabor the point.

Just as God's power is released through His trinity by its unity, so also our power and ability is in direct relation to the unity of our trinity. We are to be balanced people. Our trinity is to be submitted in order, even as God's trinity. Paul's prayer for the believer in I Thessalonians was for balance for wholeness, that the *spirit, soul,* and *body* be made whole (ischuo). This powerful word in the Greek means to be able, to have power (Kittle), even suggesting military power. Jesus said in Matthew 9:12, "They that be whole (ischuo) need not a physician." Surely the epitome of the desire of all saints is to be so whole that they have no needs whatsoever!

Medical science recognizes that most of our physical sicknesses are psychologically induced. This means that something is out of balance within us. They know that fear, hatred, resentment, jealousies, tensions, strife, etc., are at the bottom of most illnesses they treat. They know that most of the people they treat will be back again, if not for that illness, then for another one.

Though imbalance in our spirit, soul, and body may not always cause physical sickness or accidents, it can cause discouragement, depression, and disappointments. We know that if the Trinity of God were to become unbalanced or at variance one with another, the whole universe would be in trouble! So also we know that our tripartite nature is in trouble when we get out of balance.

This same balance is needed in the home between parents. It is of the utmost importance that they support each other so the children will not be confused. I Corinthians 7:14 could be alluding to this thought when Paul refers to children being unclean — when only one of the parents is saved. When the parents are both saved, then the children are holy. You will also notice in the following verse that, if the unbelieving one departs, we are not to try to stop him . . . inasmuch as their presence would then be a barrier to peace in that home. According to I Peter 3:7, prayers are hindered (ekkapto — to cut out . . . Vine) when the divine order is missing.

Inasmuch as this is not a treatise on the home, we will move on to deal with what happens in our tripartite nature when we allow one part to pull away and do its own thing. If the spirit, soul and body worked together normally and naturally and without a tendency toward disunity, Paul's prayer for their wholeness would have been unnecessary. My body is to be in submission to my soul. My soul is to be in submission to my spirit.

When we speak of our soul, we mean our emotions, will, and intellect. If I allow my body to do its own thing, go its own way, eat all it wants, sleep all it wants, play all it wants, be unsubmitted, I will have imbalance. I *will not* allow my body to eat all it wants, to indulge itself. This is why Paul, in writing to the Romans, asked them to present their bodies a living sacrifice. The body is to be sacrificed in order to worship . . . Romans 12:1 Amp.

Paul referred to his body in "keeping it under" lest he become a castaway. He would not allow his body any indulgence that would release it from submission to his whole person. There have been times I have said "no" to the invitation to have a lovely, big piece of pie. Not because it was unlawful to me, but because I just needed to "bring my body under." Next time I might say "Yes!" In that case it would be my intelligence (soul) ruling. The experts tell us that if we fill our stomachs to capacity each time we eat, the stomach will require more to fill it the next time. You can apply this principle to other lusts and cravings of the body.

Likewise my soul, especially my emotions, must be submitted to my spirit. My spirit is eternal. It is given of

God and came from Him, but needed to be born again. When it is born again by the Spirit of God, it knows all things. We know the things of God by the Spirit of God. The Spirit of God indwells our spirit *and He communicates with our spirit first, not our intelligence (soul) or emotions (soul)*.

I dare not allow my soul to do its own thing. The very first thing it probably would want to do is enjoy itself in a long, long pity-party. Oh, yes . . . it enjoys hearing itself say, "Poor me; others have it so nice."; "Some were just born lucky."; "He was born rich, and I have to work hard for everything I get."; "He is so good looking."; "She is so beautiful."; "I wish I had some talent — poor me — I was behind the door when so many good things were passed out . . . sigh!" Everyone is tempted to feel sorry for himself on occasion.

Bring your soul (suche'), its will, emotions, and intellect under subjection to your spirit. It is your spirit (heart — I Peter 3:4) with which you believe in God. You can't lay hold on eternal truths with your head! The natural man (mind) receiveth not the things of the Spirit of God — I Corinthians 2:14. When you allow your soul to dominate you, then you will have greater difficulty in praying and believing God for the answer. This is why so much of the music we hear ministers only to the soul. Music is only edifying if it is ministering the truth of God's Word. Listen to the words of the majority of hymns and gospel songs. It ministers to the weakness of the emotions, primarily to those looking for commiseration.

It is refreshing to sing so many of the scripture choruses such as, Greater is He That is in You; Beloved Let us Love One Another; A Merry Heart Doeth Good Like a Medicine; Unto Him be Glory in the Church; His Banner Over Me is Love; Seek Ye First the Kingdom of God . . .and on and on. No wonder revival is here! We are singing and ministering to the whole man!

Many of the good old hymns the early church sang were born during revival. This is true of the Martin Luther, John Wesley hymns. While some truths are eternal, some of the hymns that were born of the Spirit in that day ministered to the needs of that day. The needs of today differ. God has given a new song. It ministers today, meeting the needs of the whole man where he lives.

Bringing the soul under, to be submitted to the leading power of the spirit, requires the spirit to be very strongly developed. In most people the soul (emotions) is much stronger than the spirit, having been developed through usage. This is especially true where the worship of the church is built around emotional singing and physical antics.

Some pastors have made a specialty of ministering only to the soulish realm. Their sermons are lacking in the Word. They draw heavily on emotional illustration. They specialize in dealing with issues of the day. They use sensational sermon topics. They border constantly on the spectacular. Their preaching is enjoyed and some large churches have been built on this ministry. They are constantly giving out tasty, sweet desserts . . . but no meat.

No wonder the people who sit under this type of ministry are weak in the Word. If you bring in a teacher, one who doesn't tell either sensational stories or heart-wringing illustrations, one who doesn't jump about, one who only stays in the Word with powerful teaching and preaching . . . the people are disgruntled. They are frustrated because they don't understand the reason for their dissatisfaction. Many of these people backslide easily, only to return again to the church at the next revival. Again they repent, only to fall away, continuing the cycle. They do not comprehend the reason for their behavior. They each have a weak spirit. They want to serve God, but cannot. They need help.

Praying will be easier and simpler when we have wholeness. Praying will be more powerful as we experience unity in our trinity. We will find ourselves spending less time on our own needs and more time for the needs of others as we ourselves experience this wholeness. Let the unity of your own trinity be your main challenge. Do not be side-tracked by allowing yourself to criticize the imbalance of others. You will find keeping unity in your trinity will require your full effort. When you make your body come under your own will, when it will obey you; when you make your emotions serve your spirit, rather than your spirit serving your emotions — you will become more like the trinity of God.

A young boy of twelve had been misbehaving. He knew it would eventually lead to a hard spanking. His parents had threatened him periodically but had been too busy to give him the attention and discipline he obviously needed. At last the inevitable happened and a stern paddling was administered to the "seat of learning". As was his custom after such a time, the boy's father sat on the edge of the bed with him, hugged him and said, "You know I don't like to have to do this but you have been asking for it." The reply that came from his sobbing son teaches us all a good lesson. He said, "Thank you, dad, for spanking me." In answer to his dad's query as to why, he answered, "It had been such a long time since you whipped me that I was beginning to think you didn't love me."

Our physical body responds in much the same way. If you let it do what it wants . . . pamper and indulge it . . . you will have a constantly unsatisfied body. If you discipline it and bring it under control, it will be a much happier, healthier body. The same is true as you bring your will, intellect, and emotions under the obedience to your born-again spirit.

Your faith in prayer and in the Word will respond. You will be believing God with far less effort. The fruit of Christian experience will grow and flourish.

10

The Pray-Er

Before we begin to think about bringing an indict-
ment against God for that long list of unanswered prayers,
let us first consider carefully the pray-er and the various
categories into which he will fall. He must submit to our
scrutiny inasmuch as he was the one who sought the Lord.
He is the one who lifted up his voice in trouble and distress. He is a type of all of us; he prayed, he sought God.
Let us examine him . . . for I suspect we will find him
falling short of the mark in several ways. All pray-ers
will fit into one of many categories.

The pray-ers first category can be likened to a man
who comes, not as a free man, but as a slave, cringing
before his taskmaster. He comes before him trembling,
always fearful about the reception he will receive. What
he really fears most may not be just a brutal slap, but an
embarrassing rejection. For no one wants to experience
this.

The pray-er, in this analogy, has no relationship to
his "boss." If he does, he has earned it by tortuous, back-
breaking labor (for which he was continually chided by
his friends) and, in his relationship at its best, he is still
the slave. As a slave, his needs are many. He wouldn't
dare come and ask but only for the most urgent necessity.
If, for instance, one of his children will die if something
isn't done, a foreclosure is threatened on his house, he
sees his family hungry and going without the necessities of
life, etc., then he will come. Whatever the need, he has

very little hope. Even as he comes, hoping that he might receive something, he is believing in his heart that it will probably cost him more than he will receive. His very reluctance to come, even at any cost, is worsened by the things he heard has happened to others. He recalled a seeker who had come, surrendering everything that had ever given him pleasure, becoming totally beholden to the giver in order to receive.

Alas, so many of God's own people approach Him, coming as a slave (servant). They feel so unqualified — so unworthy to come. Somehow they always have had the picture of someone having to give up so *many good things* to get *some little thing*. You have heard of them. One of the first things such a person will say is, "I feel so unworthy. I can't live the Christian life." These expressions reveal total unawareness of any understanding of a wonderful heavenly Father who loves, cares, and is more anxious to give to you than you are to receive from Him. So what is greatly needed is a relationship that can break the "slave-taskmaster" image. The pray-ers described in the foregoing paragraphs will always have the longest list of unanswered prayers.

Pray-ers falling into the second category are the ones who approach God as man would his banker. He does have somewhat of a relationship. He has, from time to time, made some deposits into the bank. Of course, he has always withdrawn almost all he has ever put in. However, he has kept his account open by periodical visits . . . except for the times he has done it by mail. After all, when one goes in person one might have to stand in line — and you most certainly will have to dress a little more formally, etc.

This pray-er's relationship with the banker is mostly through the people who work for the bank. They seem to always know what they are doing, and they know the banker personally. Consequently he trusts them to keep good records and to handle his affairs. This is good because the pray-er never seems to be aware of the checkbook balance and attends to business affairs sloppily. He knows they will notify him if he becomes too badly overdrawn. You might even say he knows the banker personally . . . that is, he knows him by sight. He is not sure the banker knows him.

But now he needs a loan — there is an emergency. Not only is he overdrawn, i.e., he has already taken out more than he has put in, he has lost his job, and may lose his house if the banker doesn't come through. So he timidly approaches the banker for his need. Several things he knows about the banker. If he gets the loan (gets his need met) he will have to repay every dime received, plus interest. The banker will be tough, will go over all the past records of all transactions (some of which he hopes will not be remembered) and very carefully examine the collateral (what he is worth). If he receives what he needs, it will be a long hard road to travel, with a sacrifice of many luxuries and no new acquisitions in the days ahead.

The analogy shows this church member as one who can always be recognized as you listen to his prayer. "Dear Lord, you know that I haven't always been faithful, but I tried. I haven't been too bad, at least not as bad as some others you have helped." So he comes to God, with great uncertainty, some faith, but mostly doubt. This kind of pray-er will account for about one-half of the rest of the unanswered prayers.

Next we come to a higher caliber of pray-er. We will begin by using the Father/Son analogy. The Bible speaks of God as "our Father," and we are His children. One would think this to be the highest form. However, there is yet a higher relationship we will refer to later. All of us should understand what is intended when we identify God as "Father" and believers as His "children." When the Bible uses this relationship, it intends to show us a Father who *always provides;* and a child, or son, who *always receives* on the basis of relationship.

It is amazing how anyone can misunderstand such a simple analogy. I guess this misunderstanding comes through our failure to have a proper concept of our heavenly Father . . . perhaps because we have too often drawn our comparison by what we have seen of earthly fathers. We have known some such poor examples, that if God were anywhere comparable to that which we have known — we will be confused! How many times has our earthly father turned us down, for what seemed to us no good reason? He had the means at his disposal but refused us! To dare to compare our heavenly Father to an earthly father would put a great strain on the capacity of an analogy to illustrate. The attributes that God demonstrates in His relationship toward us is the epitome of what all earthly fathers should be and can be.

The pray-er will have an almost impossible task of establishing a good spiritual relationship with his heavenly Father if he hasn't experienced a healthy, loving relationship with his earthly father. Our heart staggers to think of the fathers who have exposed little children to their behavior . . . the drunkards, the wife beater, the child beater, the incestuous, etc. The analogy will suffer even more if one's father had a father who came far short of his responsibility, also thereby compounding the difficulties. What about the pray-er who has no earthly father? The one who never knew the security of parental love? Or was raised in foster homes, or by relatives?

Lastly, we have yet a higher category . . . higher than that of the Father/Son category. It is found in our text at the beginning of the chapter, and especially verse 14 that says, "Ye are my friends, if ye do whatsoever I command you." Jesus said He would no longer call you servants. The relationship is now changed. I no longer approach the throne of God as a child to his father. Though the former analogy still has great value in illustrating relationship and authority, I now have a new way to go to God. It is even better than a perfect Father/Son relationship!

I now can go to God through someone else. That "someone" is a perfect Son of a perfect Father. I, as a pray-er, now rely on that perfect relationship. I now, not by any good works of mine, can come boldly to the throne of God, "not in fear — the fear of rejection — that the servant (slave) had. It is not the uncertainty of the pray-er who approached the banker. I do not come even on any personal relationship I have with anyone . . . but I come in the name of another, one who has met all qualifications and requirements and satisfied every claim against me. One who has paid all my debts. One who took my prison sentence and served it; who took my death sentence and served it; who spanned the great distance between Deity and flesh, bridged the mighty gulf between earth's poverty and God's plentiful economy. His name is Jesus.

I simply ask the Father in Jesus' name. I no longer rhetorically say, "Our Father, which art in heaven." I say, "My father, who rules over all, I come to you in Jesus' name." Now I have someone with whom I can identify. He, Jesus, also lived in the flesh. He was tempted as we are, yet without sin. (Read related verses in Hebrews 4:14-16).

What is this new relationship made possible by the life and death and resurrection of our Lord Jesus? It is not only a Father/Son relationship, but even more. It is a friendship. No longer do we have to wonder if the throne is open to our approach. I now have a new and living way. The most blessed part is that I continue to enjoy the Father/Son relationship.

What has happened is that the child has grown up! I now sit down with my Father in a new way. A new dimension has been added. A friendship has developed, adding to the Father/Son relationship. The baby, then the child, then the teenager . . . has now developed into a full grown man. No longer does the son have to come to the Father as he once came. "At that day ye shall ask in my name: and I say not unto you, that I will pray the Father for you: For the Father himself loveth you, because ye have loved me, and have believed that I came out from God." (John 16:26, 27).

Something beautiful has developed, the same thing that developed between Abraham and God. They now have become friends (James 2:23). What a beautiful picture. We can hear God the Father, because of Jesus His Son, who says, "Son, all your friends are now my friends . . . bring them home any time you want to. Share with them all I have given to you — they are welcome."

Where then, does the pray-er miss it? Any friendship becomes strained and unproductive if there is no fellowship. Any fellowship becomes strained if all one party wants out of the relationship is material benefits. The pray-er can now have two blessed things: sweet, beautiful fellowship, and also all of his needs met. His fears are gone. He lives in confidence.

A good illustration would be to imagine a very wealthy man saying to his son, "Son, I am going to take you around the world. Our accommodations and travel will all be first class. We will eat the very best food and enjoy beautiful sights. You may bring your friends along." I am sure that the son may have to leave certain of his friends at home. They would be very uncomfortable on that voyage. These would be the ones who complain no matter how good the food is . . . always fretful about the little things. Now the son would want them to come along, but he would not force them because they would only spoil it for the rest. Except, of course they would learn to be sweet, positive, and gracious. Until then they will miss out on many trips.

Jesus is saying, "Come, be my friend . . . fellowship with me. All my Father has is yours. All you need do is use my name and your prayer will be granted. But remember, I can only call you my friends if you keep my commandments."

"Oh!" you say, "that is the catch . . . His commandments are too many!"

"No," he answers. "Just one . . . A new commandment I give unto you that you love one another, as I have loved you." (John 13:34)

Not many . . . and not unreasonable. The pray-er must assume his part in both the answer to prayer — and also the many that go unanswered.

If you feel guilty about your friendship and fellowship with Jesus, work on it, improve it. It is up to you, because He has done all He can do; *it is now up to you.*

11

Prayer Crutches

We read in Isaiah 29:13, "Wherefore the Lord said, Forasmuch as this people draw near me with their mouth, and with their lips do honor me, but have removed their heart far from me, and their fear toward me is taught (learned) by the precept of men." In Matthew 15:8 Jesus reminded the people of this great danger. Here we have a sad picture of a great nation in prayer, people kneeling before the doors of the Holy of Holies — speaking, saying, confessing all the right words, as they have learned them from the precepts of men. All of this is vain because they do not believe them. They were not speaking them out of their hearts, but just with their lips only.

It is always amazing how the human being never changes, even from millenium to millenium. Here we are in the 20th century, and we're doing the very same things. People fill our churches in perfect prayer posture before the throne of God . . . but are merely mouthing prayers. Prayers they really need to have answered — but alas, all is vain. They haven't learned that they are only rehearsing prayers. What we really need to learn is the difference between mouthing prayers and believing prayers.

There are thousands who attend great divine healing meetings. They hear great faith teachers. They learn to repeat their version of what they understood to come forth from good men. They learn, by rote, their little cliches and go away repeating them. Here are some you might

have heard, "Ah, ah, you claimed it . . . now you have it."
"Faith is not a farce, it is a force." "I refuse to claim these
symptoms." Again and again we hear the comprehending
of beautiful truths mutilated through superficial understanding. Is there anything wrong with these sayings?
Oh no, they are all good, and have been proven by many
people to be very profitable. Then what is wrong? The
wrong is in the fact that they have become mottoes, mere
sayings . . . only crutches to prayer.

Not only are many of our "mouthed" sayings mere
crutches to help our struggling faith, but they have
actually become confessions of unbelief. Someone was
heard to say, "I am just claiming a safe journey for all
of my folks. I do not believe they will have a wreck."
This can be a great expression from the heart, or could
only be words expressing a fearful, weak hope. Another
person was heard to say, "I just refuse to have this sickness that is going around." This can be a great expression
of faith . . . but it could also be an expression of a fear
that is lurking in the heart; and by saying the *right thing*
he hopes to overcome the fear. Thus his sayings become
only a crutch to help his faith.

Many have received healing by *acts* of faith. We have
heard them and have tried to imitate their same *acts*. To
the former, they were truly acts of faith, but when we try
to copy them they will not work for us. One of the more
common *acts* of faith concerns prayer for the eyes, especially if one is already wearing glasses. People relate how
when they were prayed for, they were healed and able to
immediately remove their glasses. We are careful to give
God praise for the healing, and for that person's faith.
However, when you asked God to heal your eyes, you
took off your glasses, but it wasn't with the same motive.
The former removed his glasses because, in his heart, he
knew he would no longer need them. You took yours off,

hoping you wouldn't need them. And therefore you had to put them back on again.

Another great, overlooked truth emerges here. We are not to discount the brother's healing or to take away from God's omnipotence; the truth of the matter is, his eyes were not as impaired as yours. The power of God is sufficient to heal, regardless of how great or how slight the healing is. But it does matter a great deal to you. He was ready for instantaneous healing . . . your healing may require time. You may need to continue to wear your glasses. *Wearing your glasses is no more a sign of unbelief than taking them off would be a sign of faith!* Your faith is not contingent on a pair of glasses, on or off! Your faith must be based on God's Word. You can continue to wear them, believing in your heart, and saying, "The time will come when I will not need these glasses any longer." The same truth will apply when I must make a decision as to whether or not I will continue to take my medicine. Really then, the medicine has nothing to do with my faith, whether I take it or lay it aside.

Picture with me a man praying for finances. Because he has waited too long to turn to prayer and to God, he has sunk deeply into the bog of financial debt. He heard of someone who also was in great financial need and escaped ruin by saying, "Lord, I will give you the 90% and I will keep the 10%." This other man had an exceptionally healthy relationship with God and had, for many years, been a consistent tither. The declaration of his faith in God worked for him. Anyone, however, using that convenant with God as a crutch will find it will not work for him. That would not be his faith speaking; it would merely be his desperation and would purchase nothing for him. He would be only hoping it would work for him.

Hope is not faith. Faith is *now*, hope is *future*. So many people are just "a-hoping and a-praying" all the time. They hear what great things God is doing for others, but it isn't working for them! All they have going for them is hope. Hope is important and of great value, however. Colossians 1:27b says, "Christ in you, the hope of glory." *Christ,* not hope, is your glory. Christ came in to your heart when you prayed, believed and asked Him in. Your prayers were answered. How did this work? Simply by believing in what the Word said. Your hope is based on your faith . . . not your faith based on hope.

Many good church members are not even saved as a result of this reversal of order. You hear them reply, when you ask them if they know they are saved, "I surely hope so." You then ask, "Do you believe you will go to heaven when you die?" They reply, "I hope so." When you ask someone if he believes that God will heal him, the reply is the same. "Hope so . . . maybe so . . . trust so." These can all be mere crutches. It seems as though we believe that a lot of verbiage will undergird our faith. But by saying the *wrong* thing we weaken our faith.

Hebrews 11:1 declares that "faith is the substance (title deed) of things hoped for, the evidence of things not seen." Faith, what one believes, the assurance, the confidence, realization, is the answer to all our hopes. Faith becomes substance and evidence of the answer to our needs. Sometimes that faith becomes evidence by just a simple scripture on which you are standing. Other times it may be a witness in your heart — you just plain feel good about it.

Abel's faith was evidenced by the fire consuming his sacrifice.

Enoch's faith was evidenced by his translation.

Noah's faith was evidenced by the first drops of rain that fell.

Believe for the answer to your prayer. Your faith will be evidenced by the victory that will come.

Merely to do, or say, something that has worked for others may not work for you. In fact, it may work against you. The word faith (pistis) simply means to be completely persuaded of a matter, person or thing. Confess (speak) simply means to speak out of great conviction. Confessing your faith is merely speaking that of which you are firmly persuaded. The kind of praying (asking) based on these two great truths will need no crutch, or aid of any kind. I believe it and say what I believe. Believing in God must, therefore, be based on what God says about what you are asking of Him. True, effective prayer is taking into God's presence His own words.

Repetition in prayer is not important, but continuously repeating what you *believe* about *God* is important. You may have used (as a crutch) the sayings of others, the acts of others; and they may have been said and done out of great faith (pistis — inward conviction). But when you picked up on these things they now become hindrances to your faith. *It is because you are leaning on them rather than on God.* Just saying repeatedly, "I am not going to get sick, I am not going to get sick," will not keep you from getting sick. In fact, you may even become more nauseated, because your prayers failed and you not only become sick, but are discouraged besides!

I read of an invalid lady who attended a great healing service. Friends carried her from the wheelchair into the service and she promptly informed the ones who brought her "to take the wheelchair back home — I won't need it again." She didn't need it — because the Lord, the Great Physician, healed her. Another lady, also in a wheelchair, heard what this lady did and repeated the same request about her wheelchair, but discovered she had to wait at the church until friends went home and returned with her wheelchair.

The author just recently heard from a pastor about a lady who had a very bad fall in front of his church. She severely cut her head, which was bleeding profusely, and cracked her kneecap. One of the assistant pastors hurried to her side, and when he saw the blood pouring out he said, "We must get you to a hospital immediately." She answered, "I will be all right because with His stripes I am healed." They finally persuaded her to go to the hospital to get her head stitched.

Upon arrival at the hospital, she repeated her faith to the doctor. He examined the wound in her head, put his finger into the broken place in her kneecap and said, "Both your kneecap and your skull are fractured, and I can put my finger in the broken place in your kneecap." Again she said, "Doctor, I know I will be all right because with His stripes I am healed." The Doctor proceeded to clean and sew up the head wound all the time the dear sister was muttering her faith in God. After he had stitched the flesh together, they took her down for X-rays. Not only could they not find any fractures in her skull, they took fourteen pictures (they usually only take two) of her kneecap and could find absolutely nothing wrong.

A person, hearing about this, might try the same thing if he ever faced this kind of emergency; but, you see, she spoke out of the inward conviction of her heart. Her faith (pistis) was speaking. Nothing the doctor could do or say could change that. When you really believe it, you don't need a crutch — for faith is the substance. You have what you say. You are not repeating cute cliches. You are only saying what you believe and what you believe is what God says!

A crutch can also be that which you plan to fall back upon in case your prayer isn't answered. We learned this from the world. David's sin in numbering Israel was probably intended to be a crutch for him to fall back on in case the enemy came in great numbers. God severely chastened all of Israel because of this sin. All the help your prayers need is only for you to believe. All things are possible to him that believeth.

A young couple were visiting some friends of mine. When they were ready to leave and came out to get into their car, they discovered some prankster had inserted a garden hose into their gas tank. Water was spewing out of the tank and flowing on to the ground. Not having much of this world's goods, they decided to just simply pray and trust God. Our friends later called us and said the couple drove their car home without it missing a stroke! I laughingly said, "God granted them a great miracle . . . or I would like to have that garden hose available for my car."

Both faith and prayers require action. The recipient will always find a course of action he can pursue.

12

A New Dimension In Prayer

"Men ought always to pray and not to faint." Luke 18:1

"Ask, and ye shall receive, that your joy may be full." John 16:24b

"I exhort therefore, that, first of all, supplications, prayers, intercessions, and giving of thanks, be made for all men; For kings, and for all that are in authority: that we may lead a quiet and peaceable life in all godliness and honesty." I Timothy 2:1-2

"O Sing unto the Lord a new song." Psalms 98:1a

"Let the word of Christ dwell in you richly in all wisdom: teaching and admonishing one another in psalms and hymns and spiritual songs, singing with grace in your hearts to the Lord." Colossians 3:16 (see Ephesians 5:18-19)

If one were to place in a single book all that the Bible has to say about prayer, praise and worship, he would virtually copy the whole Bible. One might as well save himself the trouble and just leave it in the Bible to be read as it is. This is not just a book on prayer. It would be a worthy book to write, but inasmuch as volumes already have been written, we will not duplicate it here. The call to prayer, the situations in which men prayed, the tremendous answers to prayer, the times men prayed

and the deliverances that came because they prayed . . .
the beauty of these, and the continuation of prayers being
prayed and answered today, would fill all our libraries.
The teachings that Jesus gave about prayer, the times
He prayed, the miracles He wrought because He was a
man of prayer, would fill a volume of books in themselves.
I cannot possibly exhaust this great subject, but permit
me to explore some new dimensions.

Before I do, may I give you another good reason why
many of the prayers prayed today do not seem to have
the same results as those recorded in the Bible? God is
first! He is "number one!" "In the *beginning God* . . . " It
all begins with Him and ends with Him. Inasmuch as God
is a God of "firsts," He places great importance in the
Bible about doing "first things first." They have to be
done first, not second, not third and not fourth. God's ways
will not work unless we proceed by His system of
priorities.

"First" is mentioned over 300 times in the Bible. The
people were instructed to "bring a lamb of the first year,"
not a lamb of the second year, or one that was old or
useless. The firstborn son was the one who received the
inheritance, not the second or third, or best looking, or
brightest. God is a God of divine order. Jesus says in Mark
3:27 that the strong man must be bound "first." In Matthew 5:24, it says that you are to be reconciled to your
brother "first," then bring your gift. Matthew 6:33 indi-
cates that you are to seek God's Kingdom "first" . . . not
after you have tried everything else, but first. In Matthew
7:5, we are to "first" cast the beam out of our own
eye, before helping our brother. Jesus told Peter to look
in the mouth of the "first" fish for the coin. On and on
you can continue in the subject of divine order as "first
things must be first." Would it not be in divine order to
call for the elders of the church first, or is it proper to go

to the doctor first, or does it matter to God which one you do first?

You might reply that you do not think that God cares whether you put Him first when you are sick. I believe it does matter, and this is why many are not healed. I believe it is an insult to God's divine order to confuse that order by not doing "first things first." Approach Him first. Approach the church first. He must be first.

This also applies to God's divine order of tithing. Tithing began before the law and continues in grace. It is God's divine design and order to bring Him the "first" fruits, the "first" tithe. To wait and see if you have anything left with which to tithe breaks God's divine order, and you will not be blessed and prospered.

When I first went into the ministry, there was an old coal miner who became converted. He heard about tithing, but when he figured up all his bills, he did not have enough left with which to tithe. So he did what everybody should do. He took out God's tithe first, then went and paid the bills and had money left over. Miscounted you say? Made a mistake in his bills? No. It was a very small miracle for God to perform. Put God first in everything. Put Him first when you wake up. Let Him be the last thing you think of at night. He is the Alpha and the Omega. The First and the Last, not the Last and the First.

In another chapter, we talked about methods of approach to the Throne of God. A prayer, Webster says, is an entreaty, an earnest request, a supplication. It can be considered a petition on the lips. When one prays, he is turning to another for help. Let us consider several ways a person can pray — not the physical approach, but the spiritual approach.

One can pray out of his emotions. The emotional approach in prayer will easily account for well over one-half of all prayers prayed. People who pray from the emotional level are praying in a time of great need or distress. This prayer need not be intellectual, for there is not time for that preparation. This type of prayer could be illustrated by the story about two men who were fishing. A storm came up and it looked as though any moment the boat would be swamped and they would perish. One man prayed: "Dear Lord, if you will save me out of this storm, I will give you $5,000.00!" They were saved. The other man overheard his companion pray that prayer. Being the head usher at the church they both attended, he kept watching for the man's $5,000. After several weeks, he said to the man, "I heard what you promised the Lord. I have been watching and you have not given the money that you promised." "Oh, that," the man replied. "I made a new deal with the Lord. I promised him $10,000 if he ever caught me in a boat again."

The intellectual prayer will follow, not really because it is better or more powerful or even more answerable. The person making the intellectual approach has thoroughly thought out all the options. He now approaches God by reason of his intelligent conclusion. The greatest weakness of this type of prayer is that it usually is based on the pray-er's self-righteousness. The Pharisee's prayer, as recorded in Luke 18:10-14, is one of the best examples one may find. His approach was one of comparison, pride and self-righteousness. On the other hand, the publican began his prayer by being cognizant of his relationship. This is the basis by which all prayers should begin.

Much time and thousands of words could be written on the other two levels of approach. There are also other approaches and stratas of prayer, such as group, congregational, etc.

The highest level, and a new dimension, in our praying is mentioned by the apostle Paul in I Corinthians 14:14: "For if I pray in an unknown tongue, my spirit prayeth, but my understanding is unfruitful." Here is a new sphere of prayer that the believer can enter into, that by-passes the mind and gets right to the heart of the matter. This is a prayer that is prayed by the born-again human spirit, through the influence and divine enablement of the Holy Spirit who gives the utterance. (Acts 2:4)

This higher dimension of prayer is what is called, in some circles, "a prayer language." This beautiful experience is missed by most theologians of the past. They interpreted Paul to be speaking against tongues in I Corinthians 14:14 because the understanding is unfruitable. If Paul, by the Holy Spirit, had gone on in verse 15 to say, "What is it then, I will not pray with the spirit at all," then most of the theologians, who miss it here, would have grounds to support their conclusion. But Paul did not say, "I will not pray with the spirit," he said just the opposite: "I will pray with the spirit" . . . i.e. without understanding.

Verse 14 clearly states that if you pray in an unknown tongue, your spirit is praying. Also supporting this is verse 2 of this same chapter 14. This clearly states that the speaker of unknown tongues "speaketh not unto men, but unto God." How clearly the Holy Spirit speaks to the church! There are the prayers of the mind, will, and intellect. But there are also the prayers that can be prayed by the Spirit, that by-pass the mind (understanding), that goes directly to God. Not only are they prayers we do not understand, but they are prayers that enter into the mysteries of God (I Corinthians 14:2b). "Howbeit in the spirit he speaketh mysteries."

Paul is so clear and precise in this 14th chapter of I Corinthians, that one does not need further proof or support. But in case someone does, all they need to do is to read Romans 8:26-27 and Jude 20. Here is how one knows for certain that they are praying in God's will. "For we know not what we should pray for as we ought." (Romans 8:26b) Many times it is impossible to know how to pray. "But the Spirit itself makes intercession for us with groanings which cannot be uttered, but through our inarticulate groans, the Spirit himself is pleading for us." (Romans 8:26 NEB)

In paraphrasing the preceding scripture, the Word is telling us that we can have a prayer language: a language that is beyond our own understanding; a language that takes our prayer life into the mysteries of God; a language that is uttered by our own spirit, by the Holy Spirit, that will improve (edify), building us up. Jude 20: "But ye, beloved, building up yourselves on your most holy faith, praying in the Holy Ghost." This is a language of prayer that will allow us to pray according to God's own will for our lives, a language too deep to be articulated by the human mind and tongue; and on even to higher dimensions. Notice that the apostle Paul said he could also sing with that same spirit; the very same prayer life we have been talking about that uses words of the spirit, can also be sung unto the Lord, by the same spirit. I Corinthians 14:15b says "I will sing with the spirit, and I will sing with the understanding also."

What is this "singing?" What is this song of the spirit? Isn't this the spiritual songs that are referred to in Colossians 3:16? Isn't this the new song that we are to sing? Isn't this a song to be sung by the barren, and even the desolate, that will cause them to enlarge their tents and break forth on the right hand and on the left; that shall remove the memory of the sin of their youth and even death? (Isaiah 54:1-4) *Here is true healing of the memory.* Here is how to live beyond the ravages of a past sinful life. Here is how to move a mountain. Here is how to enter into a new freedom of prayer and how to soar into the mysteries of the heavens. Here is a new dimension that frees the spirit of man to express himself to the Spirit of God.

Sing unto the Lord. Sing with the spirit. Sing also with the understanding. You might say, "What shall I sing?" Sing with the unknown tongue that by-passes the mind. Sing also with a song that your mind will understand, a song whose words you will recognize. It is a beautiful experience to lead a whole congregation in a new song; each one making up and composing their own new song to the Lord. Yes, it is childlike, but it is beautiful.

Do you have a mountain facing you, an over-whelming problem, and you have done everything you know to do? Then sing to it. Shout to it, speak to it; out of your spirit cry Grace! Grace! Grace! Make up a song to it and let that song be a prayer to the Lord. Sing it to the Father in Jesus' name and watch the mountain disappear. Receive the answer to your prayer.

Many people are waiting for the Lord to do something about the enemy that has come against them. It could be a marital problem, a financial problem, a sickness against their bodies. While you are waiting for the Lord to do something, the Lord is waiting for you to take action against the problem. You see, God has done all he can do about the devil. There is nothing left for him to do. God, through Jesus the Son, defeated Satan at the Cross. In II Chronicles 20:2, the enemy had come against the people of God. They fasted, they worshipped, they believed, but it was not until they sang a song of praise (Verse 22) that the enemy was defeated.

As we conclude this chapter, we might hear someone say that the Book of Corinthians was written to just emotional people, perhaps who were not deeply spiritual. They would conclude that it is only for weak saints to speak with tongues. Then read carefully Paul's admonition to those people. "If any man think himself to be a prophet, or spiritual, (if any man thinks he speaks for God or has the spirit—Beck) let him acknowledge (prove)

that the things that I write unto you are the commandments of the Lord." (I Corinthians 14:37). They are life-
giving commandments. Let us practice them daily; let us
enter that higher dimension of prayer life. Break forth
into singing, Saints. Sing with the spirit (prayer language). Sing with your own understanding.

Break forth into singing, Zion;

For He is the Lord of all the earth.

Pray at all times — on every occasion, in every sea-
son — in the spirit, with all (manner of) prayer and
entreaty. To that end keep alert and watch with strong
purpose and perseverance, interceding in behalf of all
the Saints (God's consecrated people).